Elevate Your Literature Review: Writing Review Papers that Stand Out

Unlocking the Secrets of Writing Engaging and Insightful Review Papers

Dr. JIGNYASA GANDHI

Acknowledgement

Writing this book has been an incredible journey, and it would not have been possible without the support and encouragement of many individuals.

First and foremost, I would like to express my deepest gratitude to my family, whose unwavering support and patience allowed me to dedicate countless hours to this project. Your belief in me has been my greatest source of inspiration. Thank you for your guidance, constructive feedback, and invaluable advice throughout this process.

I am also deeply thankful to my friends, who requested me for assistance in paper publication and motivated me to write this book.

Lastly, I extend my heartfelt appreciation to my readers. Your interest and engagement are the ultimate validation of my efforts. I hope this book serves as a useful and inspiring resource on your own journey.

Thank you all for being a part of this endeavor.

Dr. Jignyasa Gandhi

About Author

Dr. Jignyasa Gandhi is an academician with over 14 years of experience in the field of Computer Science & Engineering education. She holds a Ph.D. in Computer Science and Engineering from Visvesvaraya National Institute of Technology, Nagpur, Maharashtra, India. Dr. Gandhi also earned her B.E. and M.Tech degrees in Computer Science and Engineering from Rashtrasant Tukadoji Maharaj Nagpur University. With a prolific career dedicated to advancing the frontiers of computer science, Dr. Gandhi has an impressive portfolio of 27 research publications in esteemed international journals and conferences, along with 3 insightful book chapters. Her academic journey and contributions to the engineering domain reflect her commitment to fostering innovation and excellence in education. Currently, Dr. Gandhi continues to inspire and mentor the next generation of engineers, drawing from her extensive expertise and passion for research.

- **Google Scholar:** https://scholar.google.com/citations?user=QuFtg1gAAAAJ&hl=en

- **LinkedIn:** https://www.linkedin.com/in/dr-jignyasa-sanghavi-gandhi-10b72167/

- **Email:** sjignyasa8588@ gmail.com

Preface

In the world of academic writing, review papers hold a significant place. They offer a comprehensive summary and critical evaluation of existing literature on a particular topic, providing a valuable foundation for further research and insight. Writing a review paper, however, is not a simple task. It requires a clear understanding of its purpose, the ability to synthesize diverse sources, and the skill to present complex information in a coherent, structured manner. This book is designed to guide you through the intricate process of writing a review paper, whether you are a seasoned academic or just starting your research journey. The book begins by exploring the purpose and types of review papers, including systematic reviews, narrative reviews, and meta-analyses, helping you to find the best format for your research goals. Then this book guides you through selecting and defining your topic, identifying gaps in the literature, refining research questions, and conducting effective literature searches. Next focus is on synthesizing and analyzing the literature, offering strategies for critical evaluation, using conceptual frameworks, and organizing findings logically. The book provides practical advice on writing a compelling introduction, presenting the literature, and creating insightful analysis, as well as the role of pictorial representations in enhancing clarity. Refining your paper is key, with tips on improving language, style, and content, and strategies for proofreading and ensuring integrity. Chapter 6 covers tools for managing citations, references, and plagiarism checks. Chapter 7 provides guidance on selecting the right journal, navigating the submission process, and understanding peer review. Each chapter includes research activities to help you develop essential skills, whether you're writing your first review paper or refining your approach. This guide will not only help you master the writing process but also deepen your understanding of review research's role in advancing knowledge.

Contents

1. Introduction: The Role and Power of a Review Paper

In the vast world of academic research, review papers stand out as guiding lights, helping researchers find their way through an overwhelming amount of information. Like a lighthouse showing sailors the safest route, a well-written review paper brings clarity and focus, making it easier to navigate complex topics. By summarizing and connecting scattered pieces of knowledge, these papers turn chaos into a clear, meaningful story. Review papers are invaluable for both beginners and experienced researchers. They provide a big-picture view of what is known in a field, highlight key discoveries, reveal trends, and point out unanswered questions, setting the stage for new research directions.

1.1. What is a Review Paper ?

A review paper is a scholarly article that synthesizes existing research on a particular topic. Unlike original research articles, which present new findings, review papers provide a summary and analysis of previously published studies. They are critical in academia as they help to consolidate knowledge, making it more accessible and understandable. By offering a curated collection of insights and evidences, review papers help researchers, policymakers, and practitioners stay updated on the latest developments and make informed decisions based on a comprehensive understanding of the field.

1.2. Objectives of the Review

The primary objective of the review is to provide a comprehensive analysis of the current state of research in specific domain. To achieve this, the following sub-objectives are outlined:

- To categorize and evaluate major research contributions and their methodologies.

- To identify and discuss prevailing trends and emerging themes.
- To highlight existing knowledge gaps and limitations in the field.
- To propose actionable insights and future research trajectories for advancing the domain.

By addressing these objectives, the review aims to create a valuable resource for academics, industry professionals, and policymakers alike, fostering informed decision-making and innovation.

1.3. Importance of Literature Reviews

Literature reviews are the cornerstone of academic research. They play a crucial role in framing the context of new studies, providing a theoretical foundation, and justifying the need for further investigation. This continuous journey of exploration and evaluation is not merely a preliminary step, but a perpetual endeavor that enriches and evolves with each research and scholarly contribution. A well-conducted literature review demonstrates the researcher's expertise and deep understanding of the subject matter. It reveals how the current research fits into the existing body of knowledge and helps to refine research questions, hypotheses, and methodologies. Moreover, literature reviews foster academic dialogue, stimulate critical thinking, and inspire innovative approaches to problem solving.

1.4. Common Challenges in Writing Review Papers

Writing review papers is a critical skill for researchers, as it involves synthesizing existing research to provide insights, identify trends, and highlight gaps in the literature.Writing a review paper is not an easy task; it comes with its own set of challenges.

- **Choosing the Right Topic:** It can be tricky to decide on a topic that is not too broad or too narrow. A well-chosen topic should cover enough material to review but still allow the author to focus on key details.
- **Finding All Relevant Studies:** With so much research available, it is easy to miss important studies. Authors need to use reliable search methods and tools to gather all necessary information.
- **Evaluating Quality:** Not all studies are equally reliable. Authors must carefully assess the quality of the research they include to ensure their review is based on trustworthy information.
- **Organizing Information:** Bringing together data and findings from multiple studies in a clear and logical way can be challenging. It is important to group similar ideas and highlight key themes without overwhelming the reader.
- **Maintaining Clarity:** Simplifying complex ideas for the readers while keeping the content informative and accurate can be a tough balancing act.
- **Identifying Gaps:** A good review should highlight what is missing in the current research. This requires the author to think critically and point out areas where further studies are needed.

In conclusion, review papers serve as a cornerstone for synthesizing existing knowledge, providing a comprehensive overview of a topic, and identifying research gaps. Crafting an effective review paper requires a systematic approach to gathering, analyzing, and presenting information in a clear and structured manner. By adhering to best practices in research, critical evaluation, and scholarly writing, authors can create valuable resources that not only summarize current advancements but also guide future studies. This chapter has laid the foundation for understanding the importance of review papers and the key steps involved in their creation, setting the stage for a deeper exploration of the process in subsequent chapters.

Hint

1. Open Google Search or Google Scholar to begin your exploration.
2. Use targeted keywords for your search, such as:
   "AI in healthcare review paper", "Artificial intelligence in healthcare systematic review", "AI in medical domain survey".
3. Examine the selected review papers carefully by reviewing their structure. Pay close attention to the headings and subheadings to understand the organization of the content and key themes covered.
4. Analyze critical sections of the paper, including:
   - **Abstract:** To grasp the primary focus and summary of the paper.
   - **Discussion:** For in-depth insights and analysis of the reviewed studies.
   - **Conclusion:** To understand the key takeaways and synthesized findings.
   - **Future Scope:** To identify emerging trends and areas for further research.
5. **Search** latest papers when following these steps.(within 4 years)

Select the topic of your choice and search out review papers based on the topic. Carefully study each review paper, paying close attention to its structure and subsections to understand how the topic is comprehensively analyzed and organized.

2. Exploring the Purpose and Types of Review Papers

2.1. Introduction

Review papers play a vital role in research and academia, serving as a bridge between past studies and future discoveries. Review papers are integral components of the academic research process. They serve to compile, synthesize, and evaluate the existing body of literature on a given topic, offering researchers comprehensive insights into the current state of knowledge. This chapter aims to elucidate the purpose of review papers and explore the various types commonly used in scholarly research.

2.1.1. Objective of Review Papers

The main goal is to summarize and critically analyze existing research, offering valuable insights that benefit scholars, practitioners, and policymakers alike. Review papers help to:

1. **Consolidate Knowledge**: Review papers collect and organize findings from many studies, creating a clear and cohesive understanding of a topic.

   For example: Review paper 'Ocular Disease Detection Systems Based on Fundus Images: a Survey' consolidates findings from multiple studies on automated detection systems using retinal images, offering a cohesive understanding of the topic.

2. **Identify Gaps**: They highlight areas where research is lacking, identifying unanswered questions and guiding future research directions.

   For example: The same ocular disease paper identifies gaps such as the lack of research in automated detection of some ocular diseases and the need for improved algorithms for early detection, guiding future research directions.

3. **Provide Context:**: Review papers place new research within the broader scientific conversation, showing how it connects to or differs from previous work.

   For example: The paper 'Review of Smart Healthcare Systems and Applications for Smart Cities' explores how smart city infrastructure, including advancements in mobile cloud computing, ubiquitous computing, and intelligent sensor networks, can enhance healthcare services within the broader context of sustainable smart city. It highlights the role of smart healthcare in improving the quality of medical services, facilitating telecommunication between patients and healthcare providers, and tracking health using wearable devices and smartphone applications and how these developments fit into the larger goal of achieving smart city infrastructure.

4. **Inform Practice and Policy**: In applied fields, review papers can influence best practices, guidelines, and policy-making.

   For example: A review paper titled 'Review of next-generation earthquake-resistant geopolymer concrete' by Mostofizadeh, S. and Tee, K.F. summarizes transformative potential of next-generation strategies in earthquake-resistant construction. The authors emphasize specific structural designs, advanced materials, and innovative construction techniques that significantly enhance resilience. Such a review is valuable for policymakers and construction companies, helping them establish guidelines and building codes that improve safety in earthquake-prone regions.

2.2. Different Types of Reviews

2.2.1. Systematic Review

A systematic review is a methodical and reproducible process of identifying, evaluating, and synthesizing all available research on a particular question. The process involves:

1. **Defining a Clear Research Question**: Specific and focused questions are formulated to guide the review.
   For example: *'Does daily meditation reduce stress levels in adults?' This focused question guides the review by specifying the topic (meditation), the outcome (stress reduction), and the target group (adults).*

2. **Comprehensive Literature Search**: A thorough search of databases and sources is conducted to find all relevant studies.
   For example: Searching databases like PubMed, Scopus, and Google Scholar using keywords like meditation, stress reduction, and adult stress; to collect all relevant studies on the topic.

3. **Selection Criteria**: Predefined criteria are used to include or exclude studies.
   For example: Include- Studies on adults practicing meditation daily for at least 4 weeks.
   Exclude- Studies on children, occasional meditation, or stress management techniques other than meditation.

4. **Quality Assessment**: The quality of the studies included in the review is evaluated using standardized tools.
   For example: Tools like the Cochrane Risk of Bias Tool are utilized to assess the reliability and rigor of the studies. This involves verifying that the studies include essential performance parameters, such as proper control groups (e.g., comparing meditation interventions with no intervention) and the use of

validated and reliable measures for outcomes like stress levels (e.g., standardized stress scales). Such assessments ensure the credibility and robustness of the review findings.

5. **Synthesis and Analysis**: The findings from the selected studies are systematically synthesized and analyzed.
   For example: After analyzing the selected studies, finding that most show a significant reduction in stress levels with daily meditation. The results might be summarized in a table or through a narrative highlighting patterns, strengths, and limitations across the studies.

To gain a comprehensive understanding of systematic reviews, we will examine an exemplary paper titled "Ocular Disease Detection Systems Based on Fundus Images: A Survey," published in the journal Multimedia Tools and Applications in 2024. This paper serves as good reference for understanding the structure, methodology, and depth required in a systematic review.

1. **Question:** How can AI based systems enhance the early screening or detection of ocular diseases using fundus images?

2. **Comprehensive Literature Search:** The paper involves a thorough search of relevant studies and articles about ocular diseases (Diabetic Retinopathy, Glaucoma, Cataract, Age-related Macular Degeneration, Hypertensive Retinopathy and Pathological Myopia) and AI algorithms for fundus image analysis, collecting comprehensive data from standard databases Pubmed, Springer, Science Direct, Google Scholar, and other credible sources.

3. **Selection Criteria:** The paper establishes well defined boundaries for which studies are eligible for inclusion and which should be excluded.

- **Inclusion Criteria:**
  - ‣ Studies focusing on AI based detection of ocular diseases using fundus images.
  - ‣ Research detailing algorithms and their performance metrics.
  - ‣ Papers discussing traditional diagnostic methods for comparison.
- **Exclusion Criteria:**
  - ‣ Studies on ocular disease detection using other imaging techniques.
  - ‣ Medical Papers not involving AI or automated systems.

4. **Quality Assessment:** The included studies were assessed for their credibility, methodology, and relevance.
   For example:
   - Evaluating the dataset size and diversity used in AI training.
   - Checking if the algorithms' accuracy was validated against clinical benchmarks.
   - Ensuring studies had clear methodologies and reproducible results.

5. **Synthesis and Analysis:** The paper synthesizes findings by categorizing ocular diseases and linking them with Artificial Intelligence. It discusses:
   - Symptoms and traditional diagnostic approaches for ocular diseases .
   - AI advancements, including smart devices and specific algorithms and their potential for more accurate and accessible diagnostics.
   - Gaps and challenges, such as the need for advanced algorithms for early detection and addressing studies with less focused ocular diseases.

2.2.2. Narrative Review

Narrative reviews, also known as literature reviews or traditional reviews, offer a qualitative summary of research on a particular topic. Narrative reviews are like paint a broad picture of a research topic without focusing on a single question. These reviews are like an artist's sketch capturing the essence and nuances of a subject through a more flexible and interpretive approach.

1. **Broad Scope**: They provide an overview of the topic rather than answering a specific research question.

   For example: A narrative review on ' The Impact of Technology on Education' explores a wide range of topics, including online learning platforms, the role of AI in personalized learning, and the use of virtual reality in classrooms. Instead of focusing on a single question, it paints a broad picture of how technology is reshaping education.

2. **Flexible Methodology**: There is no standardized methodology, allowing for a more flexible approach.

   For example: When exploring the role of AI in healthcare, a narrative review might include a mix of academic studies, expert opinions, and real world case studies, making it rich and varied in content without sticking to a rigid structure.

3. **Critical Analysis**: Authors critically analyze the literature, often providing their interpretations and opinions.

   For example: In a review on 'The Challenges of Work from Home', the author might analyze studies showing increased productivity and others highlighting burnout. The review could include the author's perspective, suggesting that while remote work offers flexibility, it requires better policies to address mental health and work life balance challenges.

2.2.3. Meta-Analysis

A meta-analysis is a quantitative approach to reviewing the literature that combines the statistical results of multiple studies to arrive at a pooled estimate of effect size. The key steps involved include:

1. **Identification of Studies**: Similar to systematic reviews, meta-analyses start with a thorough search for relevant studies.
   For example: Suppose you want to know if regular exercise reduces the risk of heart disease. You start by searching databases like PubMed, Google Scholar, and Cochrane Library for studies that examine the effect of exercise on the incidence of heart disease in adults.

2. **Data Extraction**: Data from the included studies are extracted and standardized.
   For example: From each study you find, you extract data such as the number of participants, the type and duration of the exercise program, and the reported outcomes related to heart disease incidence (e.g. number of heart disease cases).

3. **Statistical Analysis**: Advanced statistical techniques are used to combine the results, taking into account the variability and heterogeneity among studies.
   For example: You use statistical software to combine the data from all the studies, considering differences in study design and populations. For instance, you calculate the average reduction in heart disease risk across all studies and the variability in this effect.

4. **Interpretation**: The pooled results are interpreted to provide a more precise estimate of the effect size.
   For example: You interpret the combined results to understand the overall effect of exercise on reducing heart disease

risk. You might conclude that regular exercise leads to a 20%
average reduction in heart disease risk, providing a precise es-
timate that can guide health recommendations for preventing
heart disease.

2.3. Determine the Purpose of Your Review

Before diving into writing a review, it is crucial to understand
the primary goal of your review. It will decide the structure,
content, and depth of your analysis, ensuring it meets your
objectives and fulfills the expectations of your audience. It
involves several key steps:

1. **Define Your Objectives**: Clearly state what you aim to
   achieve with your review. Are you looking to summarize
   the current state of knowledge, identify gaps, or provide
   recommendations?
   For example: You want to review how AI is improving
   diagnostic accuracy in healthcare. Your objective is: 'To sum-
   marize the current state of knowledge on how AI technologies
   enhance diagnostic accuracy and identify areas needing fur-
   ther research.'

2. **Select the Type of Review**: Choose the type of review
   that best aligns with your objectives. For instance, if you
   want to provide a comprehensive synthesis of all available
   evidences on a specific question, a systematic review might
   be appropriate. If you seek to offer a broad overview of a
   topic, a narrative review could be more suitable.
   For example: If your aim is to provide a detailed synthesis of
   all evidence on AI's effectiveness in diagnostics, a systematic
   review would be appropriate. If you want to give a broad
   overview of various AI applications in healthcare, including
   diagnostics, treatment planning, and patient management, a
   narrative review is more suitable.

3. **Consider Your Audience**: Tailor your review to the needs of your intended audience. Academic audiences may prefer systematic reviews or meta-analyses, while practitioners may benefit more from narrative reviews that provide practical insights.

   For example: If your audience consists of healthcare researchers and professionals, a systematic review that provides rigorous evidence on AI's role in diagnostics would be ideal. If your audience includes hospital administrators or healthcare practitioners, a narrative review that highlights practical applications and case studies of AI in healthcare might be more useful.

4. **Evaluate Resources and Time**: When selecting a review method, consider the time and resources availability. Systematic reviews and meta-analyses are ideal for comprehensive and rigorous analysis but both are time-consuming and resource-intensive. In contrast, narrative reviews can be completed more quickly and with fewer resources, making them a more feasible option for certain circumstances.

   For example: If you have limited time and resources, you might opt for a narrative review on the general benefits of AI in healthcare, which can be completed more quickly. If you have ample resources and time, a systematic review on the specific impact of AI algorithms on improving diagnostic accuracy could provide detailed insights and guide future research.

Review papers play a crucial role in advancing academic research by summarizing and synthesizing existing knowledge. Understanding the different types of review papers and their respective purposes is essential for researchers to effectively communicate their findings and contribute to the scientific discourse.

Select and analyze three review papers on the topic of **AI in Healthcare.** Each paper should represent a different type of review: a narrative review, a systematic review, and a meta-analysis. Answer the following questions after analyzing these papers:

1. What is the primary purpose of each review paper?
2. How does the structure and methodology differ among the three types of reviews?
3. What kind of insights or conclusions does each type of review offer?

Hint:

Select three Papers as follows:

1. **Narrative Review:** A paper summarizing key advancements in AI driven medical imaging technologies.
2. **Systematic Review:** A study analyzing the effectiveness of AI algorithms in diagnosing cardiovascular diseases, based on a predefined set of criteria.
3. **Meta-Analysis:** A statistical analysis of multiple studies measuring the accuracy of AI in detecting diabetic retinopathy.

Perform Analysis of Each Review:

1. **Narrative Review**
   - **Purpose:** Provides a broad overview of the role of AI in medical imaging, focusing on technological trends and future potential.
   - **Structure and Methodology:** Lacks a strict methodology; the author selects studies based on relevance and expertise.
   - **Insights:** Highlights emerging technologies and conceptual applications but lacks detailed quantitative analysis.

2. **Systematic Review**
   - **Purpose:** Critically evaluates the evidence supporting AI applications in cardiovascular diagnostics.
   - **Structure and Methodology:** Follows a strict protocol, including a predefined research question, search criteria, and inclusion/exclusion guidelines.
   - **Insights:** Offers a thorough and unbiased assessment of current research, identifying gaps and inconsistencies.
3. **Meta-Analysis**
   - **Purpose:** Combines quantitative data from multiple studies to assess AI's overall diagnostic accuracy in detecting diabetic retinopathy.
   - **Structure and Methodology:** Includes statistical pooling of data using tools like sensitivity and specificity analysis.
   - **Insights:** Provides statistically robust conclusions, for example AI achieving an average diagnostic accuracy of 92%.

Perform Comparison:
- **Narrative Review:** Ideal for introducing a topic and exploring broad trends.
- **Systematic Review:** Useful for rigorous evaluation of existing evidence and identifying research gaps.
- **Meta-Analysis:** Offers precise, data-driven conclusions, often influencing clinical practices and policy decisions.

> **Research Activity**
>
> Apply the same steps to your chosen topic, understand and synthesize key research findings by performing a structured review of literature related to your selected topic.

3. Research Topic Selection and Effective Literature Search

3.1. Identify Gaps in Existing Literature

In the vast ocean of academic research, identifying gaps in existing literature is a crucial step for developing a significant and impactful study. Gaps represent areas where knowledge is either missing, contradictory, or insufficient. Here's how you can effectively identify these gaps:

1. **Extensive Reading**: Immerse yourself in the current research by reading a wide range of articles, reviews, and books in your area of interest.
   For example: If you are interested in AI applications in healthcare, start by reading a wide range of articles, reviews, and books about how AI is being used in diagnostics, treatment planning, and patient management.

2. **Review Current Trends**: Look at the recent publications to understand the trends, advancements, and emerging questions in your field.
   For example: Look at recent publications on AI in healthcare to see trends, such as the increasing use of machine learning algorithms for early disease detection. Notice any emerging questions or areas that are frequently mentioned but not yet deeply explored.

3. **Analyze Critiques and Discussions**: Pay attention to the critiques and discussions sections of papers, where authors often highlight the limitations of their work and suggest areas for future research.
   For example: In a paper discussing AI for disease detection, the authors may mention that while AI shows promise, there

is limited research on its effectiveness in real-world clinical settings. This highlights a gap that you could focus on.

4. **Use Citation Analysis Tools**: Citation analysis tools such as Google Scholar and Web of Science can provide valuable insights into the frequency and context in which studies are cited, helping to identify areas that require further investigation.

   For example: By using Google Scholar, you can assess how frequently and in what contexts studies on AI in healthcare are referenced. This analysis might reveal that while there is abundant research on AI applications in radiology, there is a noticeable gap in studies focused on AI for mental health diagnostics, highlighting an area for potential exploration.

5. **Consult with Experts**: Engage with mentors, colleagues, and other experts in the field to gain insights on where significant gaps might lie.

   For example: Talk to healthcare professionals or domain experts, your professors, mentors, or colleagues who specialize in AI and healthcare. They might point out specific areas needing more research, such as the integration of AI with existing hospital information systems.

3.2. Refine the Research Question and Scope

Once you've identified the gaps, the next step is to refine your research questions and scope. Here is a structured approach to ensure your research is focused and manageable:

1. **Formulate Clear and Specific Questions**: Start by drafting broad questions and then narrow them down to be as specific as possible. A clear and specific research question will guide your study more effectively.

   For example: Broad: 'How does AI impact healthcare?'
   Specific: 'What is the effectiveness of AI algorithms in improv-

*ing the accuracy of skin cancer diagnosis compared to tradi-
tional diagnostic methods?'*

2. **Define Your Objectives**: Clearly outline the objectives of
   your study. What do you expect to achieve? This helps in
   keeping your research focused.
   *For example: The objective of this study is to determine
   whether AI algorithms can improve the accuracy of skin
   cancer diagnosis. Additionally, it aims to explore the types of
   AI algorithms that are most effective and the specific aspects
   of diagnosis they enhance (e.g. early detection, reducing false
   positives).*

3. **Set Boundaries**: Determine the scope of your research
   by setting clear boundaries on what will and will not
   be included. This could involve geographical, temporal, or
   contextual limitations.
   *For example: This research will focus on studies involving
   AI algorithms used for skin cancer diagnosis in patients aged
   18 and older, with data collected over the last five years. It
   will exclude other applications of AI in healthcare and studies
   involving other diseases.*

4. **Conduct a Feasibility Analysis**: Assess the feasibility
   of your research questions within the constraints of time,
   resources, and available data.
   *For example: Assessing feasibility involves ensuring access
   to a sufficient number of relevant studies on AI in skin cancer
   diagnosis within five years of span, availability of tools to
   measure diagnostic accuracy, and adequate time and resources
   to conduct a thorough review and analysis.*

5. **Iterate and Refine**: Continuously refine your research
   questions based on feedback from peers, mentors, and preliminary literature searches.

__For example:__ After initial feedback, the research question was refined from 'How does AI improve healthcare?' to 'What is the effectiveness of AI algorithms in improving the accuracy of skin cancer diagnosis compared to traditional diagnostic methods?' Preliminary literature search indicated a gap in studies comparing different AI algorithms, guiding the refinement process.

3.3. Databases and Keywords

Selecting the right databases and keywords is a crucial step in the research process, significantly influencing the scope and quality of the information you retrieve. Efficient and effective search strategies ensure that your research is comprehensive and based on the most relevant and credible sources. This section will guide you through the process of choosing databases and keywords strategically to enhance your research endeavors.

1. **Identifying Relevant Databases:** Different databases cover different fields of research. Identifying the correct database according to your domain is essential. Here are some commonly used databases:
   1. **PubMed:** Focuses on biomedical and life sciences literature. Being indexed in PubMed means your work is accessible to a wide audience in the medical and health sciences.
   2. **Scopus:** A comprehensive abstract and citation database covering a broad range of disciplines like engineering, science, mathematics and arts. Indexing in Scopus enhances visibility and citation potential across various fields.
   3. **IEEE Xplore:** Specializes in research related to electrical engineering, computer science, and electronics. Being indexed in IEEE Xplore means your work is recognized

and accessible to professionals and researchers in the technology and engineering fields.

4. **ScienceDirect:** A premier full-text database providing access to peer-reviewed journals, books, and articles across diverse fields like life sciences, health, engineering, and social sciences. It offers high-quality resources for research and knowledge dissemination.

5. **SpringerLink:** A global publishing platform known for its extensive collection of academic books, journals, and reference works in disciplines like science, technology, medicine, and humanities. It offers robust tools for researchers, enabling collaboration and knowledge-sharing.

6. **Google Scholar:** A broad, freely accessible web search engine that indexes the full text or metadata of scholarly literature across many disciplines. Inclusion in Google Scholar increases the discoverability and accessibility of your work to a global audience, enhancing its reach and citation potential.

7. **PsycINFO:** A comprehensive database from the American Psychological Association (APA) providing access to a wide range of scholarly articles, books, and dissertations in psychology and related fields. It covers topics such as behavioral science, mental health, neuroscience, and social sciences.

8. **JSTOR:** A digital library offering access to a vast archive of scholarly journals, books, and primary sources across a wide range of disciplines, including humanities, social sciences, natural sciences, and arts.

9. **ERIC (Education Resources Information Center):** Focuses on education related literature, including journal articles, research reports, and conference papers. Indexing in ERIC ensures that your educational research is accessible to educators, policymakers, and researchers,

supporting evidence based practice and policy in education.

Ensure the databases you choose are well regarded in your field to access high quality and relevant sources. Consider using multidisciplinary databases such as Google Scholar, Scopus, ScienceDirect, Xplore and Web of Science. These databases provide comprehensive search results across various subjects. Utilize specialized databases that focus on niche areas within your field, such as PsycINFO for psychology or ERIC for education. These databases often contain more targeted resources.

2. **Effective Keywords for Searching in Databases:** Crafting a good set of keywords is essential for effective searching. Start with broad terms and progressively use narrower terms.

   1. **Use Synonyms**: Identify the main concepts and terms related to your research topic. Include synonyms and related terms to capture a wider range of articles.
   For example: Main Term: 'AI in Healthcare'
   Synonyms: 'Artificial Intelligence in Healthcare', 'Machine Learning in Medicine', 'AI in Medicine' , 'Health Informatics', 'Digital Health

   2. **Boolean Operators**: Use Boolean operators (AND, OR, NOT) to refine your search queries. For example, using AND narrows your search by including all specified terms, OR broadens it by including any of the specified terms, and NOT excludes specific terms.
   For example: 'AI in Healthcare' AND 'Diagnostics'
   'Artificial Intelligence' OR 'Machine Learning' AND 'Health', 'AI in Medicine' NOT 'Robotics'

3. **Truncation::** Use truncation (e.g. 'psycholog*' to find 'psychology', 'psychological', etc.) and wildcard symbols to find variations of a word.
   For example: *'Diagnos*' to find 'Diagnosis', 'Diagnoses', 'Diagnostic'*
   'Technolog' to find 'Technology', 'Technologies'*

4. **Phrase Searching**: Use quotation marks for phrase searching to ensure that the search results contain the exact phrase.
   For example: *'AI in Healthcare Diagnostics', 'Machine Learning in Medicine'*

3.4. Tools and Techniques for Efficient Literature Search

Efficient collection and management of literature are critical for conducting a systematic review and ensuring that your research is based on comprehensive and credible sources. Here are some tools and techniques to streamline the literature collection process:

1. **Advanced Search Techniques**: Leverage the advanced search options provided by academic databases to streamline the search process and focus on highly relevant results. Use filters and advanced search options to narrow down results by date, publication type, subject area, etc.
   For example: When searching for AI applications in medical imaging, use PubMed's advanced search filters to narrow results by publication date (e.g. studies published in the last 5 years), publication type (e.g. reviews, clinical trials), and subject area (e.g. radiology, oncology).

2. **Snowball Technique**: Use the references of key articles to find additional relevant studies (backward searching) and check who has cited these articles (forward searching).

For example: *Start with a key article on AI in skin cancer detection. Use the references cited in this article to find additional relevant studies (backward searching). Then, check which newer articles have cited this key article (forward searching) to discover recent developments and related research.*

3. **Literature Mapping**: Visual tools like mind maps, research rabbit, concept maps,etc. can help you organize the literature thematically and identify connections between studies. *For example:* *Use a tool like ResearchRabbit to create a visual map of literature on AI in healthcare. Identify main themes such as AI in diagnostic imaging, AI in drug discovery, and AI in patient monitoring. This helps you see connections between studies and identify gaps in the research.*

4. **Alerts and Subscriptions**: You can configure alerts in databases to receive notifications about new publications in your field of interest or recent works from prominent experts in that domain. *For example:* *Set up alerts on databases like PubMed and Google Scholar for keywords like 'AI in healthcare', 'machine learning in medicine', and 'deep learning in medical imaging'. This way, you receive notifications about new publications that match your interests.*

5. **Library Resources**: Consult with librarians who can provide guidance on specialized databases and resources. Use institutional access to digital libraries and repositories for comprehensive literature access. *For example:* *Consult with your university librarian to get access to specialized databases like IEEE Xplore, which contains extensive literature on AI in healthcare technology. Use institutional subscriptions to access full text articles that are otherwise behind paywalls.*

6. **Open Access Journals**: Explore open access articles in domain journals and open access journals. These research articles are freely available.

   For example: Explore open access articles in reputed journals or completely open access journals like PLOS ONE and the Journal of Medical Internet Research (JMIR) to find freely available research articles on the latest AI applications in healthcare.

7. **Networking**: Engage with peers and experts through academic events to gain insights into ongoing research. Attend conferences, workshops, and seminars to learn about the latest research and connect with other researchers.

   For example: Attend conferences such as the AI in Healthcare Summit and workshops on healthcare technology to learn about cutting-edge research and network with other researchers and healthcare professionals in the field.

8. **Preprint Servers**: Preprint repositories provide early access to research findings. Check preprint servers like arXiv, bioRxiv, and medRxiv for early access to research findings before they are formally published.

   For example: Check preprint servers for topics like AI algorithms for diagnosing diseases and AI driven healthcare systems.

9. **Abstract and Full Text Screening**: A systematic screening process helps refine the literature pool. Start with abstract screening to filter out irrelevant papers, and then proceed to full-text screening for in-depth analysis.

   For example: Begin with abstract screening to quickly filter out irrelevant papers on AI in medical imaging. Once relevant papers are identified, proceed to full text screening for a detailed analysis of methodologies, results, and conclusions.

By employing these tools and techniques, you can streamline the literature collection process, ensuring that you gather comprehensive and relevant information for your research. This systematic approach enhances the quality and depth of your review, laying a solid foundation for your scholarly work.

Select a research topic on **AI in Healthcare** and conduct a literature search and perform the following steps:

1. **Select and Define a Specific Topic:** Narrow down the broad area of AI in healthcare to a specific research question.
2. **Identify Keywords:** Generate a list of keywords and phrases to guide your search.
3. **Conduct a Literature Search:** Use academic databases (e.g. PubMed, IEEE Xplore, Scopus) to find relevant papers.
4. **Analyze and Categorize Results:** Organize the papers into themes or categories based on their focus.

Hint:

Define the Topic:

1. **Broad Area:** AI in Healthcare
2. **Narrowed Topic:** The Use of AI for Early Detection of Alzheimer's Disease Using Medical Imaging
3. **Final Research Question:** How effective are AI based medical imaging tools in the early detection of Alzheimer's disease?

Identify Keywords:

1. **Primary Keywords:** Artificial intelligence, Alzheimer's disease, medical imaging, early detection.

2. **Secondary Keywords:** Deep learning, neural networks, diagnostic accuracy, biomarkers, MRI.
3. **Boolean Search Query:**("Artificial intelligence" OR "AI") AND ("Alzheimer's disease") AND ("medical imaging" OR "MRI") AND ("early detection")

Conduct the Literature Search:
- **Databases:** PubMed, IEEE Xplore, and Scopus
- **Search Results:** Retrieve 100 articles, Segregate based on your research question.
  - Include papers based on Alzheimer's disease diagnosis using machine learning, deep learning or some artificial intelligence techniques.
  - Exclude papers based on pure medical research based on Alzheimer's disease, patient treatments, etc.
    After the segregation process, approximately 75-80 articles will be retained, while the remaining ones will be excluded from further analysis.

Categorize the Results:
- **Identify Themes:**
  - **Technological Approaches:** Use of deep learning and convolutional neural networks or machine learning approaches or some other advance approaches.
  - **Clinical Applications:** AI's role in improving early diagnosis accuracy.
  - **Challenges and Limitations:** Ethical concerns and dataset limitations.

Apply the same steps to your chosen topic to practice narrowing down a research topic, identifying effective search strategies, and categorizing literature to build a foundation for a review paper.

4. Organization and Synthesis of the Literature

Effective literature review demands rigorous evaluation and strategic organization of sources. This chapter delves into the techniques for critically analyzing sources and using conceptual frameworks and thematic analysis to create a solid foundation for your research.

4.1. Techniques for Critical Analysis of Sources

1. **Assessing Relevance**: Ensure the source is directly relevant to your research question. Check if it addresses your specific area of interest.

   For example: If you are researching the impact of AI on diagnostic accuracy in healthcare, a study that examines the effectiveness of AI algorithms in detecting cancer from medical imaging would be directly relevant. In contrast, a study focusing on the use of AI for administrative tasks in healthcare might not be as relevant unless it discusses implications for diagnostic processes or accuracy.

2. **Evaluating Credibility**: Consider the author's credentials, the publication outlet, and the study's methodology.

   For example: If you're studying machine learning algorithms for cybersecurity, it's important to check the credentials of the author(s) and the publication outlet. For instance, a paper from an author with a strong research background in cybersecurity, published in a reputable journal would generally be more credible than one published in a lesser known, non-peer-reviewed source.

3. **Examining Methodology**: Critically assess the research design, sample size, data collection methods, and analysis techniques used in the study.

For example: *When reviewing a study on hardware acceleration for deep learning, critically evaluate the study's methodology. Check if they used a realistic dataset, such as ImageNet for image recognition, and if they tested their accelerator in varied environments. A study that only uses a small, unrepresentative dataset might not provide reliable results applicable to real-world applications.*

4. **Analyzing Findings and Conclusions**: Reflect on whether the conclusions are well supported by the data and if the findings are significant and generalizable.

   For example: *A meta-analysis of multiple studies on the impact of diet on heart disease would provide a comprehensive analysis of the data, drawing conclusions based on the combined results of the included studies. If the authors claim their study outperforms others but only tested it on limited samples, their conclusions may not be robust enough to generalize across diverse population.*

5. **Identifying Bias and Limitations**: Look for any potential bias in the study and acknowledge its limitations.

   For example: *In research on bias in face recognition algorithms, look for potential biases in the dataset used for training. If the dataset is not diverse and mostly represents certain demographics, the algorithm's effectiveness might be skewed towards those groups, highlighting a limitation in generalizability. Recognizing such biases is crucial for evaluating the reliability of the findings, especially for applications with social impact.*

4.2. Conceptual Frameworks and Thematic Analysis

1. **Conceptual Frameworks**: These provide a structured approach to categorize and interpret literature. Examples include the use of models, theories, and diagrams that relate

concepts and show relationships.

For example: In the field of psychology, the Cognitive-Behavioral Framework is widely used to understand mental health and illness. This framework posits that cognitive processes (thoughts) influence behaviors and emotions. For instance, a study might use this framework to explore how negative thought patterns contribute to depression and develop interventions to modify these thoughts to improve mental health.

2. **Thematic Analysis**: This involves identifying, analyzing, and reporting patterns (themes) within data. The steps include familiarization with data, coding, generating themes, reviewing themes, defining and naming themes, and writing up.

For example: A research project exploring first-year college students' experiences during the COVID-19 pandemic. Researchers would conduct interviews, transcribe the data, and generate initial codes like 'adaptation to online learning' and 'mental health challenges'. These codes would then be grouped into overarching themes such as 'Challenges of Online Learning' and 'Impact on Mental Health', providing a detailed qualitative analysis of students' experiences during the pandemic. This approach ensures that the study is both structured and insightful, yielding comprehensive results.

4.3. Developing a Structured Outline

Organizing your findings logically is vital for a coherent and compelling review paper. This section provides strategies for developing a structured outline that ensures clarity and cohesiveness in your review.

4.3.1. Organization of Findings Logically

1. **Chronological Order**: Presenting studies in the order they were conducted to show the evolution of research.

For example: In the field of renewable energy, you might present the evolution of solar panel technology chronologically.

Starting with the first silicon solar cell developed in the 1950s, progressing through major advancements such as the development of thin film solar cells in the 1970s, to the advent of high efficiency multijunction cells in the 2000s, and finally to the latest innovations in perovskite solar cells. This order shows how the technology has evolved over time and highlights key milestones in its development.

2. **Thematic Order**: Grouping studies by themes or topics to highlight trends and commonalities.

   For example: *In environmental engineering, you could organize your findings on water purification technologies thematically. Grouping studies by the type of purification method, such as:*

   - Physical Methods: Sand filtration, membrane filtration.

   - Chemical Methods: Chlorination, ozonation.

   - Biological Methods: Constructed wetlands, bioreactors.

   - Advanced Methods: UV radiation, nanotechnology.

   This thematic arrangement helps in understanding the various approaches to water purification and comparing their effectiveness and application contexts.

3. **Methodological Order**: Organizing sources based on the methodologies used (e.g. qualitative vs. quantitative studies).

   For example: *In the field of computer vision, you might organize research on object detection based on the methodologies used. For instance:*

   - Traditional Methods: Methods using handcrafted features like SIFT, SURF, and HOG.

   - Machine Learning Methods: Techniques utilizing support vector machines (SVM) and decision trees.

   - Deep Learning Methods: Approaches based on convolutional neural networks (CNNs) like YOLO, Faster R-CNN, and SSD.

   By organizing the sources methodologically, you highlight the progression from traditional to modern techniques and provide insights into the strengths and weaknesses of each approach.

4.4. Creating a Coherent Flow in the Review Paper

Crafting a review paper that is not only informative but also engaging requires careful planning and organization. A coherent flow ensures that your paper is easy to read and understand, allowing your audience to follow your arguments and insights seamlessly. Here is how to achieve that:

- **Introduction:** Set the stage by introducing the topic, providing background, and stating the purpose of the review.
- **Body:** Organize the main sections around the chosen structure (chronological, thematic, methodological), ensuring each section flows logically into the next.
- **Subsections:** Use subheadings to break down sections into more manageable parts, making it easier for readers to follow your argument.
- **Transitions:** Use transition sentences and paragraphs to connect ideas and sections smoothly.
- **Conclusion:** Summarize the key findings, highlight the implications, and suggest areas for future research.

A well structured outline not only aids in organizing your thoughts but also helps the reader navigate through your review with ease.

For Example:

Topic: The Impact of Artificial Intelligence on Healthcare

Introduction

Artificial Intelligence (AI) has revolutionized numerous sectors, with healthcare being one of the most significant. From early diagnosis to personalized treatment plans, AI's applications in healthcare are vast and transformative. This review paper aims to explore the current state of AI in healthcare, identify key advancements, and highlight areas for future research. By synthesizing recent studies, we will understand AI's role in improving patient outcomes and efficiency in healthcare services.

Body: Using Thematic Order for Organization

Main Sections: Diagnostic Tools, Treatment Plans, Patient Management, Ethical Concerns

- **Diagnostic Tools**
  - AI in early disease detection
  - Case studies on AI powered diagnostic systems

- **Treatment Plans**
  - Personalization of treatment using AI
  - AI in predicting treatment outcomes

- **Patient Management**
  - AI in monitoring patient health
  - Applications of AI in managing chronic diseases

- **Ethical Concerns**
  - Privacy issues in AI healthcare applications
  - Ethical implications of AI decisions in patient care

Subsections: Under "Diagnostic Tools"

- **Subsection 1:** AI in Early Disease Detection
  - Overview of AI technologies used for early detection
  - Example studies on AI in early cancer detection

- **Subsection 2:** Case Studies on AI Powered Diagnostic Systems
  - Detailed analysis of AI diagnostic systems

▸ Comparison of AI systems vs. traditional methods

Transitions:
While AI's role in diagnostics has shown significant promise, its application extends beyond disease detection. Another critical area where AI demonstrates transformative potential is in the personalization of treatment plans.

Conclusion:
AI has already begun to transform the landscape of healthcare through its applications in diagnostics, treatment personalization, and patient management. However, several ethical concerns and challenges remain. Future research should focus on addressing these ethical issues, improving the accuracy of AI systems, and expanding their applicability. By continuing to explore and refine these technologies, we can harness AI's full potential to enhance patient care and outcomes.

4.5. Information Synthesis

Synthesizing information effectively involves comparing, contrasting, and writing insightful summaries. This section explores techniques for synthesis and how to maintain depth in your summaries.

4.5.1. Techniques for Information Synthesis

1. **Comparative Analysis**: Compare and contrast different studies, highlighting similarities, differences, and trends.
   For example: Comparing different algorithms for object recognition in computer vision.
   - Study 1: Research on Support Vector Machines (SVMs) for image recognition, highlighting good performance with proper feature extraction but shows lower accuracy compared to CNNs for large datasets.
   - Study 2: Research on Convolutional Neural Networks (CNNs) showing high accuracy in image classification tasks, such as recognizing objects in the ImageNet dataset.

- Study 3: Research on transfer learning networks for image recognition, highlighting good performance for large datasets.

In a comparative analysis, you would highlight the similarities (all techniques used for image recognition) and differences (CNNs outperform SVMs on large datasets but require more computational power). Trends might include the increasing preference for deep learning models like CNNs over traditional machine learning techniques due to their superior performance on complex tasks.

2. **Integration**: Integrate findings from various studies to provide a comprehensive understanding of the topic.

   For example: Integrating findings on renewable energy sources to provide a comprehensive understanding of their environmental impacts.

   - Study 1: Examines the benefits of solar power, such as reduced greenhouse gas emissions and sustainable energy production.

   - Study 2: Analyzes wind energy, showing it significantly reduces reliance on fossil fuels but has potential impacts on wildlife.

   - Study 3: Investigates hydroelectric power, highlighting its renewable nature but noting risks to aquatic ecosystems.

   By integrating these findings, you can provide a holistic view of renewable energy sources, demonstrating that while each has unique advantages and challenges, collectively they contribute significantly to reducing carbon emissions and promoting sustainability.

3. **Critical Reflection**: Reflect on the significance of the findings, discussing their implications and contributions to the field.

   For example: Reflecting on studies investigating autonomous vehicles' impact on traffic safety.

   - Finding 1: Autonomous vehicles (AVs) have the potential to

reduce traffic accidents caused by human error.
- Finding 2: Some studies indicate that AVs may struggle with complex driving environments, leading to new types of accidents.
- Finding 3: Ethical and legal implications, such as decision-making in unavoidable accidents, remain unresolved.
In a critical reflection, you would discuss the significance of these findings, such as the overall potential of AVs to enhance traffic safety. You would also address the implications of the unresolved challenges, suggesting that further research and policy development are necessary to fully realize AV benefits while mitigating associated risks. By reflecting on these contributions, you provide a nuanced perspective on the current state and future directions of AV technology.

4.6. Crafting Deep and Insightful Summaries

1. **Conciseness**: Summarize the key points without omitting critical details.

   For example: Summarizing a study on the impact of machine learning in predicting equipment failures in manufacturing.
   - Key Points: Machine learning models, such as neural networks, can predict equipment failures with high accuracy, leading to reduced downtime and maintenance costs. The study showed a 20% increase in operational efficiency using predictive maintenance.
   - Concise Summary: Machine learning models significantly enhance the accuracy of predicting equipment failures, resulting in increased operational efficiency and reduced maintenance costs in manufacturing.

2. **Depth**: Provide enough context to make your summaries meaningful and insightful.

   For example: Providing context for a study on the use of graphene in improving the efficiency of solar panels.
   - Key Points: Graphene's superior electrical conductivity and

mechanical strength make it an excellent material for enhancing solar panel efficiency. The study demonstrated a 15% increase in efficiency compared to traditional silicon-based panels.

- Summary with Depth: Graphene, known for its remarkable electrical conductivity and strength, has shown promising results in boosting the efficiency of solar panels. By integrating graphene, researchers achieved a 15% efficiency improvement, highlighting its potential to revolutionize solar energy technology.

3. **Balanced View**: Present a balanced view by including both supporting and contradicting studies.
   For example: Summarizing research on the effects of autonomous vehicles (AVs) on traffic safety.
   - Supporting Studies: Multiple studies indicate that AVs can reduce traffic accidents caused by human error, leading to safer roads.
   - Contradicting Studies: Some studies suggest AVs may struggle with complex driving environments, potentially leading to new types of accidents.
   - Balanced Summary: While autonomous vehicles have the potential to enhance traffic safety by reducing human error related accidents, challenges remain in navigating complex driving environments, which could introduce new types of risks. Thus, further research is necessary to address these concerns.

4. **Original Analysis**: Include your analysis and interpretation to add value beyond mere description.
   For example: Analyzing studies on the impact of renewable energy adoption on grid stability.
   - Findings: Solar and wind energy integration can pose challenges for grid stability due to their intermittent nature. However, advancements in energy storage technologies and

smart grid systems can mitigate these issues.
- Original Analysis: The integration of solar and wind energy into the power grid presents stability challenges due to their variability. However, the development of advanced energy storage solutions and smart grid technologies offers a viable path forward, ensuring a stable and reliable energy supply while promoting sustainable energy practices.

By synthesis these techniques, a review paper will present the existing research and also offers new insights and perspectives.

Your task is to organize and synthesize the literature you have collected on AI in Healthcare. Follow these steps:

1. **Create a Literature Matrix:** Develop a table to organize key details of each paper (e.g. authors, year, focus, methodology, findings).
2. **Identify Themes:** Group the papers into thematic categories based on their focus (e.g. applications, challenges, future directions).
3. **Synthesize Findings:** Write a concise synthesis of the findings for one theme, highlighting commonalities, differences, and gaps in the research.
4. **Visual Representation:** Create a visual summary (e.g. concept map or flowchart) to illustrate relationships among the themes.

Hint:

Literature Matrix:

Author(s)	Year	Focus	Methodology	Findings
ABC et al.	2020	AI in medical imaging for diagnostics	Deep learning applied to MRI	Achieved 95% accuracy in detecting brain tumors.
XYZ et al.	2021	AI in predictive analytics for diseases	Machine learning algorithms	Early detection of diabetes with 88% precision.
PQR et al.	2022	Challenges in AI adoption in healthcare	Survey based analysis	Lack of standardized datasets is a major barrier.
BCD et al.	2019	AI's impact on patient care efficiency	Case study in hospitals	Reduced diagnosis time by 30% in emergency settings.
LMN et.al.	2023	Ethical issues in AI driven diagnostics	Qualitative review	Concerns about bias and patient data privacy are prevalent.

Identifying Themes:
- Theme 1: Applications of AI in Diagnostics
- Theme 2: Challenges in AI Adoption
- Theme 3: Ethical and Privacy Concerns

Synthesis of Findings (Theme 1: Applications of AI in Diagnostics): AI has proven highly effective in diagnostic applications, particularly in medical imaging and predictive analytics. ABC et al. (2020) demonstrated that deep learning models achieve high accuracy in detecting brain tumors from MRI scans, while XYZ (2021) showcased AI's ability to predict diabetes early with considerable precision. Additionally, BCD et al. (2019) highlighted AI's practical benefits, reducing diagnosis time in emergency settings. However, these advancements rely heavily on high quality data, which may not always be available across healthcare systems.

Visual Representation: A concept map is a visual tool that helps to organize and represent knowledge, making it easier to understand and communicate complex information. Here's an example of a concept map focused on "AI in Healthcare," illustrating its various branches and sub branches.

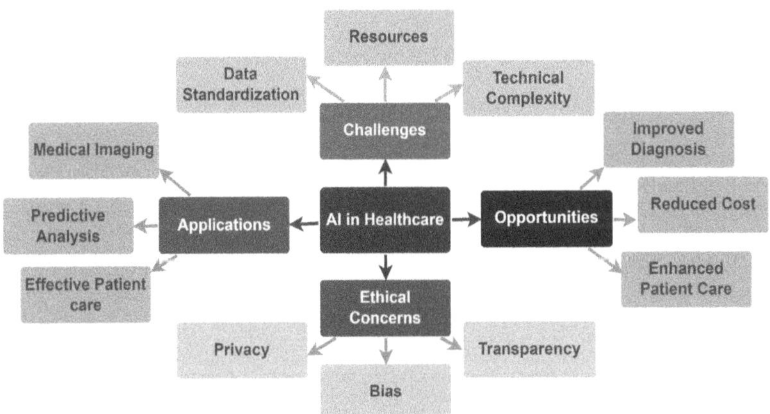

Figure 1: Concept Map Example

Apply the same steps to your chosen topic to practice organizing and synthesizing literature to identify patterns and gaps, which will help in constructing a well structured review paper.

5. Writing the Review Paper

Writing a review paper is a fundamental skill in academic research. A well crafted review paper not only synthesizes existing knowledge but also provides new insights and perspectives that can guide future research. This chapter will guide you through the key elements of writing an impactful review paper.

5.1. Build Foundation with Impactful Introduction

The introduction sets the stage for your review paper, capturing the reader's attention and establishing the foundation for your analysis.

1. **Importance of the Review**: Start by providing background information on the topic. Explain why this area of research is important and relevant. Highlight any recent advancements or significant findings that make the review timely.

   For example: In recent years, artificial intelligence (AI) has significantly impacted healthcare, offering innovative solutions for diagnosis, treatment, and patient management. This review aims to explore the latest developments in AI applications in healthcare and their implications for future research and practice.

2. **Defining Scope, Purpose, and Structure for Readers**: Clearly outline the scope of your review, the purpose of your analysis, and the structure of your paper. This helps readers understand what to expect and how the review is organized.

   For example: This review focuses on AI's applications in healthcare, including diagnostic tools, treatment planning, and patient management. The paper is structured into three main sections: an overview of AI technologies, a discussion of their applications in healthcare, and an analysis of ethical considerations.

5.2. Effective Presentation of the Literature

Effectively presenting the literature involves organizing studies in a way that highlights their significance and contributions to the field.

1. **Methods for Grouping Studies**: Organize the studies using a logical structure, such as chronological order, thematic order, or methodological order.
   For example: Grouping studies on AI in healthcare thematically:
   - Diagnostic Tools
   - Treatment Planning
   - Patient Management

2. **Writing Clear and Cohesive Literature Summaries**: Summarize each study concisely, focusing on key findings, methodologies, and relevance to your review. Ensure that your summaries are clear and cohesive, linking studies together to create a narrative.
   For example: <Author_name> ABC et al. (2020) demonstrated that AI algorithms could accurately diagnose skin cancer from images, achieving an accuracy rate of 95%. Similarly, <Author_name> XYZ et al. (2021) applied AI to radiology, where it significantly reduced diagnostic errors.

5.3. Insightful Analysis and Discussion

Developing insightful analysis and discussion is a critical part of any research paper. This section is where you provide your critical insights, draw connections between different studies, and highlight the broader implications of your findings. Here are some strategies for crafting an effective analysis and discussion:

1. **Identifying Patterns, Themes, and Gaps**: Identifying patterns, themes, and gaps in the literature is crucial for insightful analysis. This process allows you to synthesize information meaningfully, highlighting trends and areas needing further investigation.

   For example: When reviewing studies on AI's role in healthcare, you might notice recurring themes such as AI's impact on diagnostic accuracy, patient management, and treatment personalization. Identifying these common threads helps to organize your discussion around key topics.

2. **Highlighting Gaps and Contradictions**: Identify areas where research is lacking or results are inconsistent.

   For example: You may find that while many studies highlight the benefits of AI in diagnostic accuracy, there are few that explore its long term reliability or the ethical implications of AI decision making. Pointing out these gaps can pave the way for future research.

3. **Synthesizing Information**: Combine findings from various sources to create a comprehensive understanding.

   For example: If multiple studies show that AI improves diagnostic accuracy by 90% for certain conditions, you can synthesize this information to argue that AI holds significant potential for early disease detection across the healthcare industry.

4. **Critical Evaluation**: Critically evaluate the methodologies of the studies you review.

   For example: If a study claims high accuracy for an AI diagnostic tool but has a small sample size or lacks diversity in its sample, discuss these limitations and how they might affect the findings' generalizability.

5. **Connecting to Broader Implications**: Discuss how your findings fit into the larger context of healthcare innovation.
   For example: If AI improves diagnostic accuracy, it might lead to earlier and more precise treatments, ultimately enhancing patient outcomes and reducing healthcare costs.

6. **Providing Original Insights**: Beyond summarizing existing research, add your own interpretation and insights.
   For example: You might suggest that the integration of AI with current diagnostic practices could be optimized through targeted training for healthcare professionals or by developing standardized protocols for AI use.

7. **Drawing Meaningful Conclusions**: Conclude by summarizing the key points of your analysis, highlighting the importance of your findings, and suggesting areas for future research.
   For example: Conclude that while AI shows great promise in healthcare, further studies are needed to address ethical concerns and ensure its safe and effective integration into clinical practice.

8. **Conclude and Recommend Future Research:** Your conclusion should summarize the key findings of your review and provide recommendations for future research.
   1. **Summarizing Key Findings**: Briefly recap the most important findings from your review.
      For example: This review highlights the significant advancements in AI applications for healthcare, particularly in diagnostic tools, treatment planning, and patient management.

2. **Providing Recommendations and Highlighting Research Opportunities**: Offer recommendations for future research and identify potential areas for further investigation.

   For example: Future research should focus on the ethical implications of AI in healthcare, the development of robust data privacy measures, and the long term impact of AI on patient outcomes. Additionally, studies exploring the integration of AI with other emerging technologies could provide new insights into its potential applications.

5.4. Pictorial Representations in Review Papers

Pictorial Representations play a vital role in review papers, helping to clarify complex information, illustrate relationships, and enhance overall readability. Pictorial representations, such as graphs, charts, tables, and diagrams, play a crucial role in enhancing the clarity, comprehensibility, and impact of review papers. They help in visually summarizing complex information, making it easier for readers to grasp key concepts and findings. For exemplary use of visual aids, the journal Advanced Drug Delivery Reviews provides outstanding references.

5.4.1. Importance of Pictorial Representations

- **Clarity and Understanding:** Visual aids help to distill complex data and findings into more understandable formats. They can simplify intricate concepts, making them accessible to a broader audience.

- **Efficient Communication:** Graphs and charts can convey a lot of information quickly, saving readers time and effort. They highlight trends, patterns, and relationships that might not be immediately apparent in textual descriptions.

- **Enhanced Engagement:** Visual elements make the review paper more engaging and appealing. They can capture the reader's attention and maintain interest throughout the document.

- **Highlighting Key Points:** Diagrams and infographics can emphasize the most important aspects of the research, ensuring that critical information stands out.

5.4.2. Types of Pictorial Representations

- **Flowchart:** A flowchart is a visual representation of a process or system, using symbols and arrows to depict the sequence of steps involved. It helps in organizing information, making complex processes easier to understand, and providing a clear path for decision-making or problem-solving.

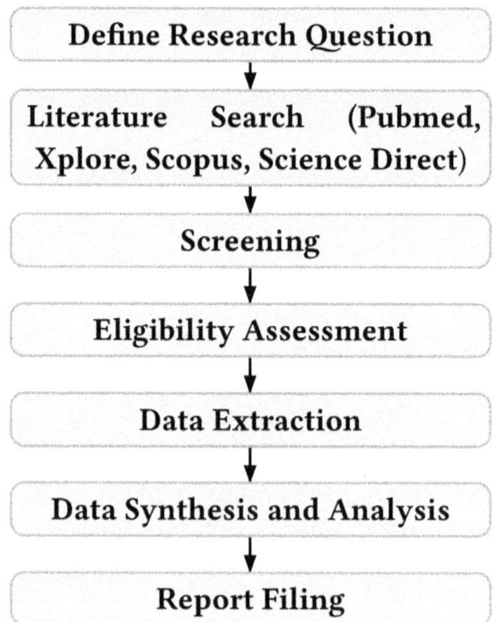

Figure 2: Flowchart outlining the general steps involved in writing a review paper

- **Pie Chart**: A pie chart is a circular graph divided into slices to illustrate numerical proportions or percentages of a whole.

Each slice represents a category, with the size of the slice corresponding to the proportion of that category in relation to the total. Pie charts are commonly used in data analysis to visually convey the distribution of data, making it easier to understand the relative sizes of different segments at a glance.

For example: *A pie chart representing the distribution of research focus areas within AI applications in healthcare in (%).*

Graph 1: Pie chart

- **Line Graph**: A line graph is a type of chart used to display data points over a continuous range, often representing changes over time. It uses a series of connected points, or 'data markers', which are plotted on a coordinate plane and linked by straight lines.

For example: *A line graph depicting the trend of AI research publications in healthcare over the past decade.*

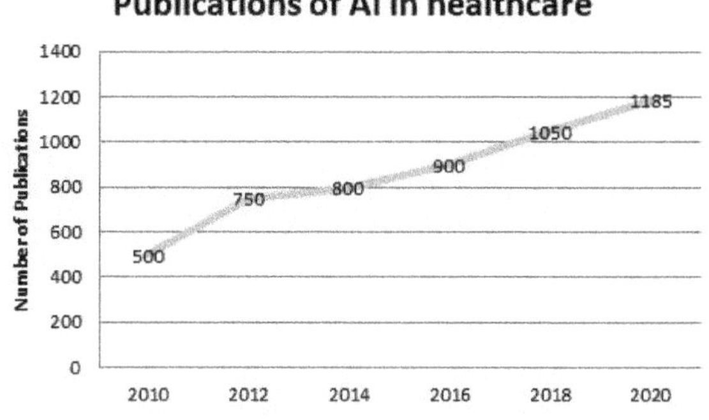

Figure 3: Line Graph for AI research publications

- **Bar Graph**: A bar chart is a graphical representation of data where rectangular bars are used to represent the values of different categories. The length or height of each bar is proportional to the value it represents, making it easy to compare the sizes of different categories.

  For example: *A bar graph comparing the performance of different machine learning algorithms in predicting equipment failures.*

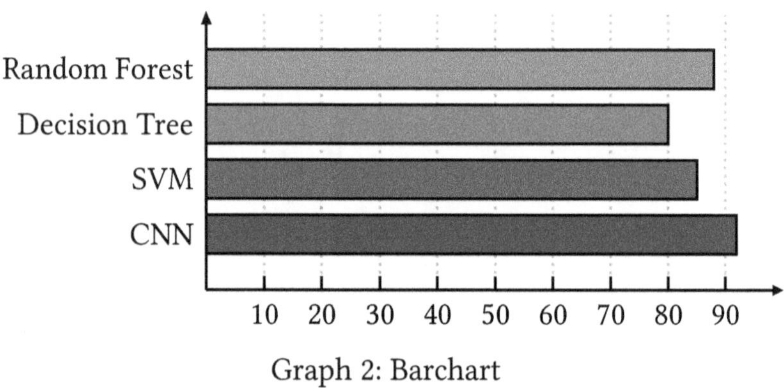

Graph 2: Barchart

- **Summary Table**: A summary table is a concise representation of data, typically used to provide an overview of key information or findings.

  For example: *A summary table comparing key findings from different studies on AI applications in healthcare.*

Author(s)	Focus Area	Key Findings	Sample size	Conclusion
ABC et al. (2020)	Diagnostic Tools	AI algorithms can diagnose skin cancer with 95% accuracy	1,000	High accuracy in diagnostics

XYZ et al. (2021)	Radiology	AI reduces diagnostic errors in radiology by 20%	500	Significant reduction in errors
LMN et al. (2022)	Patient Management	AI improves chronic disease management efficiency	200	Enhanced efficiency in patient care

- **Infographic**: An infographic is a visually engaging representation of data or information, designed for easy comprehension. In research papers, it often serves as a graphical abstract, summarizing key findings in a concise, visual format.

For example: Clara Cestonaro et al. emphasize the integration of AI algorithms in medical diagnostics in their review paper 'Defining medical liability when artificial intelligence is applied on diagnostic algorithms: a systematic review'. The central theme of their research is visually represented in their graphical abstract. The following figure presents the infographic, outlining both the advantages and disadvantages of AI in healthcare.

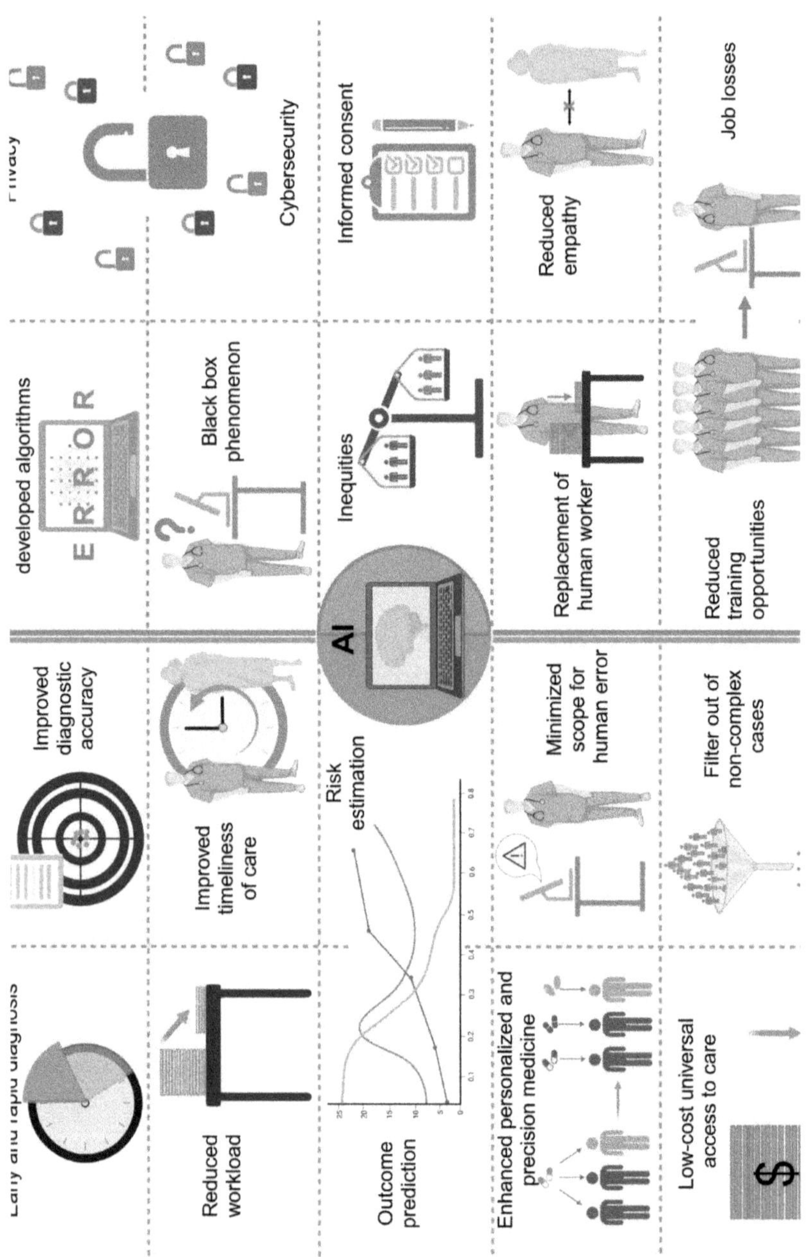

Figure 4: An infographic summarizing the advantages and challenges of using AI in healthcare.(Image Courtesy: Frontiers in Medicine. 10. 10.3389/fmed.2023.1305756)

Writing an effective review paper involves crafting a strong introduction, presenting the literature clearly, developing insightful analysis, and providing meaningful conclusions and recommendations. By following these steps, you can produce a review paper that not only synthesizes existing knowledge but also contributes new insights to the field.

Draft a review paper with focus on exploring the role of AI in the diagnosis of Alzheimer's Disease (AD). Complete the following steps:

- **Define the Scope:** Choose a specific aspect of AI in Alzheimer's diagnosis, such as its use in medical imaging or predictive analytics.
- **Write the Introduction:** Provide a brief background on Alzheimer's Disease and the significance of AI in its early detection.
- **Synthesize Literature:** Summarize and synthesize findings from at least three studies, integrating evidence effectively.
- **Conclude and Identify Gaps:** Conclude the section by summarizing insights and highlighting challenges or research gaps.

Hint:

1. **Title:** AI Applications in Early Detection of Alzheimer's Disease Using Medical Imaging
2. **Introduction**

    Alzheimer's Disease (AD) is a progressive neurodegenerative disorder and a leading cause of dementia worldwide. Early detection is critical for effective intervention, yet traditional diagnostic methods often fail to identify subtle changes in the brain associated with early stage AD. Artificial intelligence (AI), particularly through advanced medical imaging techniques such as MRI and PET scans, has emerged as a powerful tool for identifying biomarkers of AD at early stages. This section reviews recent advancements in AI applications for medical imaging in Alzheimer's diagnosis, synthesizing key findings and identifying areas for future research.

3. **Synthesis of Literature**

AI has demonstrated significant potential in enhancing the accuracy and efficiency of Alzheimer's diagnosis. For example, ABC et al. (2021) utilized a convolutional neural network (CNN) to analyze MRI scans, achieving an accuracy of 94% in detecting early-stage Alzheimer's. Similarly, LMN (2022) employed a deep learning model to process PET scan data, identifying amyloid plaque buildup with a sensitivity of 92%. In a comparative study, XYZ et al. (2023) highlighted that AI based tools not only outperform traditional diagnostic methods but also reduce analysis time by 40%, enabling earlier intervention. Despite these advancements, these studies emphasize the need for diverse datasets, as current models are often trained on homogeneous populations, limiting their generalizability.

4. **Conclusion and Research Gaps**

AI driven medical imaging tools have shown remarkable promise in the early detection of Alzheimer's Disease, offering high accuracy and efficiency. However, challenges such as limited data diversity, lack of standardized evaluation metrics, and ethical concerns surrounding patient data privacy remain barriers to widespread adoption. Future research should focus on creating more inclusive datasets and developing interpretable AI models to ensure equitable and transparent healthcare solutions.

Apply the same steps to your chosen topic to practice structuring and writing sections of a review paper.

Define a scope, write introduction, synthesize literature and conclude with identifying research gaps.

6. Polishing the Review Paper

6.1. Refining Your Paper

6.1.1. Review the Content for Clarity and Coherence

1. **Importance of clarity and logical flow:** Clarity and logical flow are essential in ensuring your paper is easily understood by readers. Clear writing eliminates ambiguity, making it straightforward for readers to grasp your arguments. Logical flow connects your ideas smoothly, guiding readers through your thought process seamlessly. This coherence is crucial for maintaining the reader's interest and effectively communicating your research findings.

2. **Techniques for improving readability:** Improving the readability of your writing is essential to ensure that your message is clear, engaging, and easily understood by your audience. Whether you're writing a research paper, an article, or any other form of content, the following techniques can help you enhance readability:

    1. **Organize your structure:** Use headings and subheadings to break up sections and guide the reader.
    2. **Simplify complex sentences:** Break long sentences into shorter ones to improve clarity.
    3. **Use transition words:** Employ words like "therefore," "however," and "moreover" to show relationships between ideas.
    4. **Active voice:** Prefer the active voice over the passive to make sentences clearer and more direct.
    5. **Consistent terminology:** Use the same terms consistently to avoid confusing the reader.
    6. **Avoid jargons:** Use simple, clear language to ensure your writing is accessible to a wider audience.

6.1.2. Enhancing Arguments and Evidence

1. **Strengthening your paper with supporting points**: Ensure your paper is clear, concise, and arguable. Strengthen your paper by providing robust evidence and well reasoned arguments. Each supporting point should directly relate to and support your paper, forming a cohesive argument throughout your paper.

   For example: If your paper is about the impact of AI on healthcare, ensure your paper is clear, concise, and arguable by stating your thesis upfront: 'AI is revolutionizing healthcare by improving diagnostics, treatment, and patient care.' Strengthen your paper by providing robust evidence, such as case studies of AI applications in radiology for improved diagnostic accuracy and examples of AI driven telemedicine platforms enhancing patient access to care.

2. **Ensuring robust and credible evidence:** In academic research and scholarly writing, the robustness and credibility of evidence are paramount. Ensuring that your evidence is both reliable and valid enhances the quality of your work and supports the conclusions you draw. Here are key strategies to ensure robust and credible evidence in your research:

   - **Use reputable sources:** Cite peer-reviewed journals, books, and authoritative websites.
   - **Provide sufficient evidence:** Back up each claim with multiple pieces of evidence to reinforce your arguments.

     For example: If arguing that AI improves diagnostic accuracy, include data from multiple studies showing reduced error rates in AI assisted diagnoses with statistics.
   - **Critically evaluate sources:** Assess the reliability and relevance of each source, considering factors like author expertise, publication date, and source credibility.

     For example: An article titled "AI-based pipeline for early screening of lung cancer: integrating radiology, clinical, and genomics data" published in The Lancet Digital Health journal. The article is authored by Ullas Batra, a Senior Consultant and Chief of thoracic Medical Oncology with more than 15 years of experience in cancer research and treatment. The author's extensive background and expertise in oncology and AI technology suggest that the information provided is highly credible and reliable. The article was published in May 2024. Given the rapid advancements in AI technology, the recent publication date ensures that the information is upto date and incorporates the latest research findings and technological developments. The Lancet Digital Health is a highly respected peer-reviewed medical journal known for its rigorous editorial standards and high impact factor. It specializes in publishing cutting-edge research on digital health technologies. The credibility of The Lancet Digital Health as a publication indicates that the article has undergone thorough peer review and editorial scrutiny, enhancing its reliability.

- **Integrate evidence effectively:** Seamlessly incorporate quotes, data, and references into your narrative to support your points without disrupting the flow.

6.1.3. Language and Style Improvements

Effective writing relies not only on the content but also on how that content is presented. Improving language and style can significantly enhance the readability, engagement, and impact of your writing. Here are some key techniques for refining your language and style:

1. **Grammar and punctuation checks:** Proper grammar and punctuation are fundamental to the readability and professionalism of your paper. Common checks include:
   - **Subject-verb agreement:** Ensure subjects and verbs agree in number.
   - **Punctuation:** Use commas, semicolons, and periods correctly to clarify meaning.

- **Spelling:** Check for and correct any spelling errors.
- **Tense consistency:** Maintain the same verb tense throughout your paper to avoid confusion.

2. **Style consistency and academic tone:** Maintaining a consistent style and academic tone is crucial for credibility and readability.

   1. **Formal language**: Use formal language appropriate for academic writing, avoiding slang and colloquialisms.
      For example: Informal: 'The study looks at how cool the new drug is.'
      Formal: 'The study examines the efficacy of the new drug.'

   2. **Third-person perspective**: Generally, use the third person language to maintain an objective tone.
      For example: First-person: 'I believe this method is effective.'
      Third-person: 'This method is considered effective.'

   3. **Avoiding bias**: Write impartially, ensuring that all viewpoints are fairly represented.
      For example: Biased: 'Clearly, the best solution is to implement this policy immediately.'
      Impartial: 'Research suggests that implementing this policy may yield positive results.'

   4. **Consistency in citation**: Use the same citation style throughout your paper, adhering strictly to the chosen format's rules.
      For example: Inconsistent: 'The results are supported by ABC (2020) and also by another study by XYZ (2019).'
      Consistent: 'The results are supported by ABC (2020) and XYZ (2019).'

6.2. Proofreading Strategies

Proofreading is an essential step in the writing process that ensures your work is polished, error-free, and ready for your audience. Effective proofreading requires a systematic approach and keen attention to detail.

6.2.1. Effective proofreading techniques

- **Take a break:** After writing, take a break before proofreading to see your work with fresh eyes.
- **Read aloud:** Reading your paper aloud helps you catch errors that you might miss when reading silently.
- **Use a Checklist:** A proofreading checklist ensures that you systematically check for specific types of errors.
- **Focus on one type of error at a time:** Concentrate on specific types of errors (e.g. grammar, punctuation) in each read-through.
- **Change the Format:** Changing the format of your document can help you see your work from a new perspective and spot errors more easily.
- **Use digital tools:** Tools like Grammarly or spell-checkers can help identify errors you might overlook.
- **Proofread Multiple Times:** Multiple rounds of proofreading increase the likelihood of catching all errors.

6.2.2. Common errors

- **Typos and spelling mistakes:** Ensure all words are correctly spelled.
- **Grammar and punctuation:** Check for correct usage of commas, periods, and other punctuation marks.
- **Consistency:** Verify that terms and style are consistent throughout the paper.
- **Formatting issues:** Ensure headings, fonts, and spacing adhere to guidelines.

6.2.3. Peer Review and Feedback

Peer review and feedback are critical components of the academic and professional writing process. They serve as mechanisms for ensuring the quality, accuracy, and validity of research and written content. Here are some of the benefits of peer review:

1. **Fresh perspectives**: Peers can provide new insights and identify weaknesses you might have missed.
   For example: You might believe your argument for the use of AI in diagnostics is comprehensive, but a peer review reveals that you overlooked the ethical implications. This new insight allows you to address this critical aspect, strengthening your paper.

2. **Quality improvement**: Constructive feedback helps improve the clarity, coherence, and overall quality of your paper.
   For example: Constructive feedback from a peer might suggest rephrasing certain sections for better clarity. For instance, instead of saying 'AI can sometimes diagnose diseases', you rephrase to 'AI has demonstrated a significant capability in diagnosing diseases and reducing error rates.'

3. **Validation**: Positive feedback from peers can validate your arguments and methodologies, boosting your confidence.
   For example: Positive feedback from a peer confirms that your methodology for collecting data on AI's impact in healthcare is robust, giving you confidence that your approach is sound and the results are valid.

4. **Incorporating feedback effectively**: Accept feedback with an open mind, even if it's critical.
   For example: A peer criticizes your literature review for lacking depth. Instead of feeling defensive, you acknowledge

the feedback and expand your review to include additional sources and a more thorough analysis.

5. **Categorize feedback**: Sort feedback into categories (e.g. major revisions, minor edits) to tackle changes systematically.

   For example: You receive feedback suggesting both major revisions (e.g. restructuring your argument) and minor edits (e.g. correcting typos). By categorizing these, you systematically address the most critical changes first, ensuring a comprehensive revision process.

6. **Implement changes thoughtfully**: Consider each piece of feedback carefully and make revisions that enhance your paper without compromising your original intent.

   For example: A peer suggests a new section on the future implications of AI in healthcare. You consider this feedback and decide to add this section, as it enriches your paper without deviating from your original thesis.

6.3. Essential Tools

6.3.1. Paper Formatting Tools

Paper formatting tools are invaluable for students, researchers, and professionals who need to ensure their documents adhere to specific formatting guidelines. These tools help streamline the process of formatting academic papers, dissertations, thesis, and other documents by providing templates, styles, and automated formatting features. Here are some popular paper formatting tools:

1. **Microsoft Word:** Microsoft Word is widely used for writing and formatting documents. It offers numerous templates for academic papers, including APA, MLA, and Chicago styles. With its built-in formatting options, you can easily adjust margins, spacing, headings, and citations. Word also allows

you to create a table of contents, insert footnotes, and generate bibliographies, making it a comprehensive tool for academic writing.

2. **Google Docs:** Google Docs is a popular online word processor that allows for real-time collaboration. It offers basic formatting tools and templates, which can be customized to fit specific formatting guidelines. Google Docs is particularly useful for group projects and collaborative writing, as it allows multiple users to edit and comment on a document simultaneously. It also integrates seamlessly with Google Drive for easy storage and sharing.

3. **LaTeX:** LaTeX is a typesetting system commonly used for scientific and technical documents. It provides precise control over document formatting, making it ideal for complex papers that include mathematical equations, tables, and figures. LaTeX uses plain text markup language and offers various templates for formatting according to different journal and conference standards. While it has a steeper learning curve, LaTeX is highly customizable and widely used in academia.

4. **Overleaf:** Overleaf is an online collaborative LaTeX editor. It combines the power of LaTeX with the convenience of cloud based collaboration. Overleaf offers templates for numerous academic journals and conferences, allowing multiple authors to work on a document simultaneously. It also provides real-time preview, version control, and easy integration with reference management tools like Zotero and Mendeley.

5. **Typst:** Typst is a modern typesetting system designed for simplicity and ease of use, targeting writers who need a flexible yet straightforward way to format their documents.

It utilizes a Markdown-inspired syntax, making it accessible to those familiar with basic markup languages. Typst offers powerful features for creating structured documents, including support for sections, figures, tables, and mathematical equations. It provides a range of templates suitable for various document types, ensuring professional and polished outputs. While easier to learn than traditional systems like LaTeX, Typst maintains a high degree of customization, making it a versatile tool for both beginners and experienced users.

6. **Scrivener:** Scrivener is a writing tool designed for long form writing projects. It provides robust organizational features, allowing writers to break their work into sections and rearrange them easily. Scrivener supports various formatting options and can compile documents into different formats, such as PDF, Word, and LaTeX. It is especially popular among authors, researchers, and anyone working on complex writing projects.

6.3.2. Citation and Reference Management Tools

Citation and reference management tools are essential for researchers, academics, and students to organize their references and manage citations efficiently. These tools provide a seamless way to collect, organize, and format citations in a variety of styles, ensuring that your academic papers adhere to proper referencing guidelines. Here are some popular citation and reference management tools:

1. **EndNote:** EndNote is a powerful reference management tool that allows users to create, manage, and format citations and bibliographies. It integrates with word processing software like Microsoft Word, making it easy to insert citations and generate bibliographies in various styles. EndNote also offers features for organizing references, sharing libraries

with colleagues, and importing references from online databases.

2. **Mendeley:** Mendeley is both a reference manager and an academic social network. It helps users organize research, collaborate with others online, and discover the latest research in their field. Mendeley provides tools for importing papers, highlighting and annotating PDFs, and generating citations and bibliographies in different styles. It also offers a desktop application and browser extension for seamless integration with research workflows.

3. **Zotero:** Zotero is a free, open source reference management tool that helps users collect, organize, and cite research sources. Zotero automatically senses content in your web browser, allowing you to add it to your personal library with a single click. It supports a wide range of citation styles and integrates with word processing software for easy citation insertion. Zotero also offers cloud storage for syncing references across devices and sharing libraries with collaborators.

6.3.3. Plagiarism Checking Tools

Plagiarism checking tools are essential for maintaining academic integrity and ensuring that all written work is original and properly cited. These tools help students, researchers, and professionals detect and prevent plagiarism by comparing submitted texts against a vast database of sources, including academic papers, books, websites, and other published materials. Here are some popular plagiarism checking tools:

1. **Turnitin:** Turnitin is one of the most widely used plagiarism detection services in educational institutions. It scans student submissions against an extensive database of academic papers, articles, and online content. Turnitin provides

detailed similarity reports highlighting any matching or similar text, allowing instructors and students to review and address potential plagiarism. It also offers features for grading and providing feedback on assignments.

2. **iThenticate:** iThenticate is a plagiarism detection tool designed for researchers, publishers, and professionals. It is commonly used by academic journals, publishers, and research institutions to check manuscripts for originality before publication. iThenticate compares texts against a vast database of scholarly articles, books, and web content, providing detailed similarity reports to ensure the integrity of academic work.

3. **Grammarly:** Grammarly is a comprehensive writing assistant that includes a plagiarism detection feature. It checks texts for plagiarism by comparing them against billions of web pages and academic papers stored in ProQuest's databases. Grammarly also provides suggestions for improving grammar, punctuation, style, and tone, making it a versatile tool for enhancing overall writing quality.

4. **Copyscape:** Copyscape is primarily used for checking web content for plagiarism. It allows users to enter URLs or paste text to check for duplicate content across the internet. Copyscape is widely used by website owners, bloggers, and content creators to ensure their content is original and not being duplicated elsewhere online. It also offers a premium service with additional features like batch search and private indexing.

5. **Quetext:** Quetext is a user-friendly plagiarism detection tool that offers both free and premium services. It uses advanced algorithms to scan documents and highlight any instances of plagiarism. Quetext provides a detailed report

with matching sources and a plagiarism score, helping users identify and correct potential issues. The premium version offers deeper searches and additional features like citation assistance.

Refining and polishing your paper is a vital step in the writing process. Ensuring clarity and coherence, rigorously revising and editing, and adhering to proper formatting and ethical guidelines will enhance the quality and impact of your review paper. Using tools like LaTeX, Overleaf, and Microsoft Word for formatting your scientific paper ensures a professional and organized presentation. Plagiarism checking tools like Turnitin, Grammarly, iThenticate, Copyscape, and Quetext help maintain the integrity and originality of your work. By integrating these tools into your writing process, you can produce high quality, original, and well formatted research papers that meet the standards of academic and scientific publications.

You have written a draft of a review paper on AI applications in diagnosing Alzheimer's Disease. Your task is to refine, format, and ensure the integrity of the paper before submission. Follow these steps:

- **Refining the Content:** Revise your draft for clarity, coherence, and conciseness. Ensure the introduction, body, and conclusion flow logically.
- **Formatting:** Format the paper according to the guidelines of a target journal, such as ensuring proper citation style (e.g. APA, IEEE).
- **Checking for Integrity:** Use tools to detect plagiarism, verify citations, and ensure all sources are properly credited.
- **Peer Review Simulation:** Exchange your revised paper with a peer for feedback, focusing on clarity, depth, and adherence to guidelines.

Hint:

Refining the Content

- **Draft Excerpt (Before Refining):** 'AI tools like CNNs are used to analyze imaging data and identify Alzheimer's biomarkers. These tools are good at early detection and perform better than traditional methods'
- **Refined Version:** 'AI driven tools, particularly convolutional neural networks (CNNs), have emerged as effective technologies for analyzing medical imaging data to identify biomarkers of Alzheimer's Disease. These models excel in early detection, consistently outperforming traditional diagnostic methods in terms of accuracy and efficiency.'
- **Revisions Made:** Improved clarity, added specificity, and enhanced academic tone.

Formatting: Ensure the document adhered to APA Style, including:

- Proper in-text citations (e.g. ABC et al., 2021).
- A well formatted reference list with consistent citation styles.
- Structured sections with appropriate headings (e.g. Introduction, Literature Review, Discussion, Conclusion).
- Used double spacing and standard font (e.g. Times New Roman, 12 pt).

Checking for Integrity

- Check the paper through plagiarism detection software (e.g. Turnitin) to ensure originality.
- Cross verify all citations, ensuring sources matched the claims made in the text.
- Include DOIs or URLs for all references to improve accessibility.

Peer Review Simulation

- Share the refined paper with a peer for feedback.
- **Peer Feedback:**
  1. Peer suggested breaking down a long paragraph in the literature review for better readability.
  2. Peer recommended to provide more examples to illustrate the challenges of AI adoption in diverse populations.
- Implement feedback by restructuring paragraphs and adding an example of dataset diversity challenges.

Final Version Highlights

- **Clarity:** Enhanced readability with concise and precise language.
- **Formatting:** Fully compliant with journal guidelines, improving professionalism.
- **Integrity:** Ensure proper attribution and originality, strengthening the paper's credibility.

- **Feedback Integration:** Addressed peer suggestions, improving depth and balance.

Perform same steps on your chosen topic to practice refinement of a research paper, ensure academic integrity, and prepare it for submission to a journal.

7. Journal Selection and Paper Submission

Selecting the right journal for your research is a crucial step in the publication process. The significance of this choice cannot be overstated, as it affects your research's visibility, the audience it reaches, and your career progression. Submitting your paper to a suitable journal enhances the likelihood of acceptance and maximizes the impact of your work. This chapter will guide you through the considerations for selecting an appropriate journal and the steps for submitting your paper effectively.

7.1. Search the Potential Journals

In the world of academic publishing, selecting the appropriate journal for your research paper is a crucial step that can significantly influence the visibility, impact, and reception of your work. This section will guide you through the process of identifying journals that align with your research focus, reviewing their aims and scope, understanding their target audience, evaluating their impact factors and reputation, and utilizing tools like Journal Citation Reports. By following these steps you can effectively identify journals that are a good fit for your research:

1. **Identify Journals that Align with Your Research Focus:** Begin by listing key journals in your field that regularly publish articles related to your topic. Look at your references and see where similar research has been published. Examine recent issues of these journals to understand the type of research they publish and to confirm that your work fits within their scope.

2. **Review the Journal's Aim and Scope:** Each journal provides an 'Aims and Scope' section on its website. This section outlines the journal's focus, the types of manuscripts it accepts, and its intended contributions to the field. Ensure that your manuscript aligns with these stated aims. Submitting a paper that does not fit the journal's scope is a common reason for rejection.

3. **Understand the Target Audience:** Identify who the journal's readership is: researchers, practitioners, policy makers, or a combination of these. Your paper should be written in a manner that addresses the interests and needs of this audience. Analyze the style, tone, and level of complexity in articles published by the journal to match your writing accordingly.

4. **Evaluate the Journal's Impact Factor and Reputation:** Journal impact factor, provided by sources like Clarivate's Journal Citation Reports, indicate the average number of citations to recent articles published in the journal. However this is not the only measure of quality, a higher impact factor often suggests a well regarded journal within its field. Consider the journal's reputation, which can be assessed through word-of-mouth, recommendations from colleagues, and review articles.

5. **Use Tools like Journal Citation Reports:** Tools like Journal Citation Reports offer insights into a journal's impact factor, subject category rankings, and other metrics. These reports can help you identify high-impact journals that align with your research. Utilize these tools to compare journals and make an informed decision about where to submit your manuscript.

6. **Verify Authenticity:** Always verify the authenticity of a journal before submitting your manuscript. Check the journal's website URL carefully, consult the journal's listing in official databases like the Scopus, Web of Science, Pubmed, Directory of Open Access Journals (DOAJ) or Journal Citation Reports, and seek advice from colleagues or mentors. Some of the fraudulent methods are as follows:

   - **Cloned Journals:** Cloned journals are fraudulent journals that imitate legitimate journals, often with similar names and website designs, to deceive authors into submitting their work and paying fees. To verify whether a journal is a cloned journal, you can visit the following website and check: https://ugccare.unipune.ac.in/Apps1/User/Web/CloneJournals.

   - **Red Flags:** Be wary of journals that have suspiciously fast acceptance times, lack peer review, or request high publication fees without clear justification.

   - **Unsolicited Emails:** Researchers receive aggressive emails soliciting manuscript submissions. Be careful with these emails and verify properly before submitting your manuscript.

7. **Use Journal Finder Tools:** To streamline the process of selecting a suitable journal, various journal finder tools are available. These tools use algorithms to match your manuscript with relevant journals based on your title, abstract, and keywords.

7.2. Journal Finder Tools

Journal finder tools are invaluable resources for researchers seeking to identify suitable journals for their manuscripts. These tools analyze the content of your abstract and provide tailored recommendations for journals that have previously published similar research. This streamlines the submission process by helping researchers target journals that are likely to be interested in their work, thereby increasing the chances of acceptance.

Steps for Using a Journal Finder Tool
- **Access the Tool:** Visit the journal finder tool's website (e.g. Elsevier Journal Finder, Springer Journal Suggester).
- **Input Information:** Enter your manuscript's title, abstract, and relevant keywords.
- **Review Recommendations:** The tool will generate a list of potential journals, along with information such as impact factor, acceptance rate, and time to publication.
- **Evaluate Options:** Compare the suggested journals based on their relevance to your research, impact factor, and other criteria important to you.
- **Choose a Journal:** Select the journal that best fits your manuscript and proceed with the submission process.

7.3. Assess the Publication Frequency and Timeline

1. **Publication Frequencies (Monthly, Quarterly, etc.):** Journals vary in how frequently they publish issues. Some are monthly, providing a steady flow of new research, while others might be quarterly or even less frequent. A monthly journal offers more frequent opportunities for publication, which might be preferable if you're seeking a faster publication timeline. In contrast, quarterly or biannual journals might have a more selective and prestigious editorial process.

2. **Review and Publication Timeline:** The timeline from submission to publication can vary significantly between journals. This timeline includes the initial review by editors, peer review process, revisions, and final publication. Investigate typical review times by checking the journal's website or contacting the editorial office. Some journals are known

for their rapid turnaround times, while others might take longer due to a thorough review process. Keep in mind your own deadlines. If you need your research published quickly, consider journals with shorter review periods.

3. **Balance Urgency with Journal Prestige:** Sometimes there's a trade-off between the speed of publication and the journal's prestige. High-impact journals often have longer review and publication timelines due to their rigorous review processes. If visibility and prestige are crucial for your career or research impact, you might opt for a higher prestige journal even if it means waiting longer for publication. Conversely, if timing is critical (e.g. due to funding deadlines or thesis requirements), you may prioritize faster publication.

7.4. Open Access or Subscription based Journals

When it comes to publishing your research, one of the critical decisions you need to make is whether to submit your work to an open access journal or a subscription-based journal. Both options have their own advantages and disadvantages, and the choice depends on your specific goals and needs.

1. **Open Access Journals**: These journals signify a revolutionary change in the academic publishing world, dedicated to democratizing access to knowledge and expediting the dissemination of research findings. Unlike traditional subscription-based journals, open access journals make scholarly articles freely accessible to anyone with an internet connection, thus removing financial barriers and vastly extending the reach of academic work.

   Following are some of the advantages:

   1. **Wide Accessibility:** Open access journals provide free, immediate access to your research for anyone with an internet connection. This maximizes the visibility and

reach of your work. Researchers, practitioners, policy-makers, and the general public can access your findings without any subscription barriers.
2. **Increased Citations:** Studies have shown that open access articles tend to receive more citations than sub-scription-based articles. The wider audience can lead to greater academic impact.
3. **Public Good:** Open access supports the principle of making research freely available to all, promoting knowl-edge sharing and collaboration.
4. **Compliance with Funders:** Many funding agencies and institutions require or encourage researchers to publish in open access journals to ensure that publicly funded research is accessible to the public.

Some of the disadvantages of open access journals are:
1. **Publication Fees:** Open access journals often charge article processing charges (APCs) to cover the costs of publication. These fees can be substantial and may not be affordable for all researchers. Some institutions or grants may cover APCs, but this is not always the case.
2. **Quality Concerns:** There are concerns about the quality and credibility of some open access journals, particularly predatory journals that prioritize profit over rigorous peer review.

2. **Subscription based Journals:** These journals have been a cornerstone of academic publishing for decades. These journals typically require readers or institutions to pay a subscription fee to access their content, ensuring that the journal can maintain high standards of quality and sustain-ability.
Following are the advantages of subscription journals:
1. **Established Reputation:** Many subscription-based journals have a long history and are well respected in

their fields. Publishing in these journals can enhance the credibility and prestige of your work. These journals often have high impact factors and rigorous peer-review processes.

2. **No Author Fees:** Typically, authors do not have to pay publication fees for subscription-based journals, as the costs are covered by subscriptions and institutional access.

3. **Access to Professional Networks:** Subscription-based journals are often associated with professional societies and organizations, providing access to a network of experts and opportunities for professional development.

4. **Rigorous Peer Review:** These journals typically conduct thorough peer review processes, ensuring that only high-quality and scientifically sound research is published. Peer reviewers are often experts in the field, providing valuable feedback to authors and maintaining the integrity of the journal.

Some of the disadvantages of Subscription based journals are:

1. **Limited Accessibility:** Access to subscription-based journals is restricted to individuals or institutions that can afford the subscription fees. This can limit the reach and impact of your research. Researchers in low-resource settings may not have access to your work.

2. **Delayed Access:** There may be delays in making your work available to the public due to the publication process and embargo periods.

3. **Cost to Institutions:** The cost of subscriptions can be high, placing a financial burden on academic institutions and libraries. Budget constraints may limit the number of subscriptions they can afford.

3. **Making the Decision:** When deciding between open access and subscription-based journals, consider the following factors:
   - **Audience:** Who is the target audience for your research? If broad accessibility and public engagement are important, open access may be the better option.
   - **Impact:** Consider the potential for increased citations and visibility with open access versus the prestige and credibility associated with established subscription-based journals.
   - **Costs:** Evaluate the financial implications, including potential APCs for open access and the availability of funding to cover these costs.
   - **Quality:** Ensure that the journal, whether open access or subscription-based, maintains high standards of peer review and academic integrity.
   - **Funder Requirements:** Check if your funding agency or institution has specific requirements or preferences for open access publishing.

7.5. Adhere to the Author Guidelines

Following the author guidelines of the selected journal is very crucial step. These guidelines outline specific requirements for formatting, structure, and content, ensuring consistency and professionalism in submissions. Following these guidelines demonstrates your attention to detail and respect for the journal's standards, increasing the likelihood that your manuscript will be considered for review rather than rejected for non-compliance.

7.5.1. Standard Formatting and Submission Guidelines

- **Formatting:** Journals often specify requirements for font type and size, margins, line spacing, and section headings. Commonly, Times New Roman, 12-point font, and double spacing are standard.

- **Structure:** The typical structure includes title page, abstract, keywords, introduction, methods, results, discussion, conclusion, acknowledgments, references, and any appendices.
- **References:** Citation style (APA, MLA, Chicago, etc.) and formatting guidelines for in-text citations and reference lists.
- **Figures and Tables:** Guidelines for the submission of figures and tables, including resolution, file formats, and captions.
- **Supplementary Materials:** Requirements for submitting any additional files or data that support the manuscript.

7.5.2. Preparing Manuscript as per Guidelines

- **Read the Guidelines Thoroughly:** Before starting your manuscript, read the journal's author guidelines carefully to understand all requirements.
- **Create a Checklist:** Make a checklist of the formatting and submission requirements and use it to review your manuscript before submission.
- **Use Templates:** Many journals provide templates that you can download and use to format your manuscript correctly.
- **Maintain Consistency:** Ensure consistency in style, terminology, and formatting throughout your manuscript.
- **Proofread:** Proofread your manuscript multiple times to catch any formatting or typographical errors.

7.6. Submitting the Paper to selected Journal

Submitting your research paper to an academic journal involves several crucial steps. Each step ensures that your manuscript meets the journal's standards and enhances its chances of being accepted for publication. Steps for entire submission process is described below:

1. **Cover Letter:** Draft a concise cover letter that outlines the main contributions of your research, its relevance to the journal's audience, and why it is a good fit for the journal. Address the editor respectfully and include any relevant information about prior submissions or related work.

2. **Manuscript:** Organize your manuscript into the prescribed sections (e.g. abstract, introduction, methods, results, discussion). Ensure that tables, figures, and references are formatted correctly. Double check that your manuscript meets the journal's word count and formatting specifications.

3. **Submit Online:** Most journals use online submission systems. Access the journal's online submission portal. Complete all required fields and upload the manuscript, cover letter, and any additional files (e.g. figures, supplementary data). Ensure all files are correctly formatted and named as per the journal's instructions.

4. **Complete Submission Forms:** Provide additional information required by the journal during the submission process. Fill out submission forms, which may include information about authorship, conflicts of interest, ethical approvals, and funding sources. Ensure all sections are completed accurately.

5. **Supplementary Materials:** Provide any additional files, such as datasets, multimedia content, or appendices, that support your manuscript.

6. **Acknowledge Submission Confirmation:** Confirming that your manuscript has been successfully submitted. You will receive a confirmation email from the journal acknowledging receipt of your submission. Save this email for future reference. Note any assigned manuscript ID or tracking number.

7.7. Peer Review Process

The peer review process is a cornerstone of academic publishing, ensuring that research articles meet the necessary standards of quality, validity, and originality before they are published. It involves the evaluation of a manuscript by experts in the relevant field who assess the work's rigor and contribution to the discipline. Here is a simple guide to understand the peer review process:

1. **Initial Screening:** The author submits their manuscript to a journal for consideration. The journal's editorial office conducts an initial screening to ensure the submission fits the scope of the journal and adheres to the submission guidelines. Manuscripts that do not meet these criteria may be rejected at this stage.

2. **Editorial Review:** The editor-in-chief or handling editor performs a preliminary review to assess the manuscript's relevance and quality. The editor evaluates the manuscript's originality, significance, and overall quality. If the manuscript passes this initial assessment, it proceeds to the peer review stage. If not, it may be rejected or sent back to the author for revisions.

3. **Selection of Reviewers:** Qualified experts in the relevant field are chosen to review the manuscript. The editor identifies and invites potential reviewers based on their expertise, availability, and any potential conflicts of interest. Typically, two to four reviewers are selected to provide a balanced evaluation.

4. **Review Process:** Reviewers critically assess the manuscript's content, methodology, and contribution to the field. Reviewers read the manuscript and provide detailed feedback on various aspects, including:
   - **Scientific Validity:** Assess the robustness of the methodology and the validity of the results.
   - **Originality:** Evaluate the novelty and contribution of the research to the field.
   - **Clarity and Coherence:** Examine the clarity of writing, logical flow, and coherence of arguments.
   - **Ethical Considerations:** Ensure that the research adheres to ethical standards and guidelines.

- Reviewers typically use a structured form or guidelines provided by the journal to submit their feedback and recommendations, which may include:
    - **Accept:** The manuscript is ready for publication with minor or no revisions.
    - **Revise:** The manuscript requires minor or major revisions before it can be accepted.
    - **Reject:** The manuscript is not suitable for publication in its current form or does not meet the journal's standards.

5. **Author Revisions:** Authors should respond to reviewers' comments and revise the manuscript accordingly. This may involve rewriting sections, adding new data, or clarifying points. The revised manuscript is then resubmitted to the journal along with a detailed response letter outlining how each comment was addressed.

6. **Editorial Decision:** The editor makes the final decision based on the reviewers' feedback and the author's revisions. The editor reviews the revised manuscript and the reviewers' comments. The possible outcomes are:
    - **Accept:** The manuscript is accepted for publication.
    - **Minor Revisions:** Further minor changes are required before acceptance.
    - **Major Revisions:** Substantial changes are needed, and the revised manuscript may undergo another round of review.
    - **Reject:** The manuscript is not accepted for publication.

7. **Publication:** The accepted manuscript is prepared for publication. The manuscript undergoes final editing, formatting, and typesetting by the journal's production team. The author may be asked to review proofs to ensure accuracy. Once finalized, the article is published in the journal.

7.7.1. Benefits of the Peer Review Process

- **Quality Control:** Peer review ensures that only high-quality, scientifically sound research is published.
- **Expert Feedback:** Authors receive constructive feedback from experts, which can enhance the quality and impact of their work.
- **Validation:** The peer review process provides a form of validation and recognition from the academic community.
- **Improved Credibility:** Peer-reviewed publications are generally considered more credible and reliable.

7.7.2. Challenges of the Peer Review Process

- **Time-Consuming:** The process can be lengthy, delaying the publication of research findings.
- **Subjectivity:** Reviewer biases and variability in reviewer expertise can affect the consistency of the reviews.
- **Transparency:** Some argue that the traditional blind review process lacks transparency. Open peer review models are being explored to address this issue.

Understanding the peer review process helps authors navigate the submission and review stages more effectively, improving their chances of successful publication and contributing valuable research to their field

7.7.3. Different Types of Peer Review

1. **Single-Blind Review:** Reviewers know the identity of the authors, but authors do not know who the reviewers are. This is the most common type of peer review.

2. **Double-Blind Review:** Neither the reviewers nor the authors know each other's identities. This helps to prevent bias based on the author's identity.

3. **Open Review:** Both the reviewers and authors know each other's identities. This can promote transparency and accountability but may also introduce bias.

7.7.4. Addressing Peer Review Feedback

1. **Prepare for Review:** Submit a well prepared manuscript that adheres to the journal's guidelines. Ensure clarity, coherence, and completeness. Include a cover letter that briefly explains the significance of your work and why it fits the journal's scope.

2. **Respond to Feedback:** Be open-minded and receptive to criticism. View feedback as an opportunity to improve your work. Address all reviewer comments systematically. Provide clear and concise responses, indicating how you have revised your manuscript in response to each point. If you disagree with a reviewer's comment, explain your reasoning respectfully and provide evidence to support your position.
Example:
Reviewer's Comment: The section on predictive analytics lacks detail on recent advancements and key studies. Additionally, the discussion on ethical concerns is brief and needs more depth, particularly regarding privacy and bias in AI systems. The lack of discussion on XYZ algorithm significantly weakens the manuscript.
Author's Response: Thank you for your valuable feedback. We have addressed your comments as follows:
   1. **Detail on Recent Advancements in Predictive Analytics**
   We have expanded the section on predictive analytics to include recent advancements and key studies in the field of AI in healthcare. This includes discussing new algorithms and their applications in predicting patient outcomes.
   Added Text: Recent advancements in predictive analyt-

ics have leveraged deep learning techniques to improve the accuracy of patient outcome predictions. Notable studies include ABC et al. (2023) who developed a neural network model that significantly enhances early detection of sepsis, and XYZ et al. (2022) who implemented machine learning algorithms to predict patient readmissions with high precision.

2. **Expanded Discussion on Ethical Concerns:**

   We have significantly expanded the discussion on ethical concerns to provide a more in-depth analysis of privacy and bias issues in AI systems. This includes recent cases and measures being taken to mitigate these concerns.

   Added Text: Privacy and bias are critical ethical concerns in the deployment of AI systems in healthcare. AI algorithms often rely on large datasets that contain sensitive patient information, raising issues of data privacy and security. Furthermore, biases inherent in the training data can lead to biased outcomes, disproportionately affecting certain patient groups. Recent efforts to address these issues include the implementation of federated learning techniques to enhance data privacy and the development of bias detection and mitigation frameworks.

3. **Lack of discussion on XYZ algorithm:**

   We appreciate the reviewer's suggestion. However, our study focuses on comparing the ABC and DEF algorithms, which are underrepresented in the literature. While XYZ is significant, it has been well covered in prior research. To maintain our paper's originality, we have added a brief mention and relevant citations of XYZ instead of a detailed analysis.

You have completed your research paper titled "**Advancements in AI for Early Detection of Alzheimer's Disease**" Your next step is to select a suitable journal for submission and prepare your manuscript accordingly.

1. **Without Journal Finder Tool:**
   - Search potential journals manually.
   - Identify at least three journals that align with your topic.
   - Consider factors like the journal's scope, impact factor, audience, and publication timeline.
   - Prepare your submission based on the selected journal's author guidelines.

2. **With Journal Finder Tool:**
   - Use a journal finder tool (e.g. Elsevier Journal Finder, Springer Journal Suggester) to search for journals based on your title and abstract.
   - Compare the suggestions and select a journal.
   - Adjust your paper formatting and structure according to the selected journal's submission requirements.

Hint:

Without Journal Finder Tool:

1. Research journal databases (e.g. PubMed, Scopus) or use Google Scholar to find journals publishing on AI in healthcare or Alzheimer's Disease.
2. Identify journals such as:
   - Journal of Biomedical Informatics
   - Artificial Intelligence in Medicine
   - Ophthalmology and Visual Science
3. Visit each journal's website to review their scope, target audience, and author guidelines.

4. Format the paper according to the chosen journal's requirements, e.g. citation style, word limit, and figure formats.

With Journal Finder Tool:
1. Input the paper title and abstract into Elsevier's Journal Finder.
2. Review the top suggestions, such as:
   - Computers in Biology and Medicine
   - IEEE Journal of Biomedical and Health Informatics
3. Compare the journals based on factors like impact factor and publication speed.
4. Select a journal, download their author guidelines, and revise the paper for submission accordingly.

> **Research Activity**
>
> You have created research paper on your choosen topic. Perform all the steps on your research paper and understand the process of journal finding with and without journal finder.

8. Conclusion: Elevating Your Review Paper

Recap of Key Steps to a Stand-Out Review Paper

Writing a review paper is both an art and a science—requiring meticulous planning, critical thinking, and a passion for discovery. Successfully navigating the journey from selecting a research topic to submitting your paper to a journal involves a series of carefully considered steps. As we conclude this guide, let's revisit the steps that can transform your work into a standout review paper while inspiring confidence in your ability to contribute meaningfully to your field.

1. **Select and Define Your Topic:** Choose a relevant and focused topic. Identify gaps in the existing literature, refine your research questions, and define the scope and purpose of your review.

2. **Conduct Effective Literature Search:** Use strategic keywords and choose the right databases (e.g. PubMed, IEEE Xplore, ScienceDirect, SpringerLink) to collect comprehensive literature. Utilize tools for efficient literature collection and management.

3. **Formulate a Research Question:** Develop a clear and focused research question that guides your study. This question should be specific, measurable, and relevant to your field.

4. **Evaluate and Organize Sources:** Critically analyze your sources for relevance, credibility, and methodology. Use conceptual frameworks and thematic analysis to organize the literature logically.

5. **Develop a Structured Outline:** Organize your findings chronologically, thematically, or methodologically. Ensure a coherent flow with clear transitions and well defined sections.

6. **Synthesize Information Effectively:** Compare and contrast different studies, integrate findings, and provide critical analysis. Identify patterns, themes, and gaps in the literature to draw meaningful conclusions.

7. **Ensure Clarity and Coherence:** Write clearly and concisely, using transition phrases to maintain cohesion. Revise and edit your paper meticulously to enhance clarity and eliminate errors.

8. **Format, Citations, and Ethical Considerations:** Follow general journal structure and guidelines, ensure proper referencing, and avoid plagiarism. Address ethical considerations and ensure compliance with submission requirements.

9. **Check for Cloned or Predatory Journals:** Verify the legitimacy of journals using tools like the Directory of Open Access Journals (DOAJ), UGC-care list or Beall's List. Cross-check journal credentials, publisher reputation, and ISSN numbers to avoid cloned or predatory journals.

10. **Journal Finders:** Journal finder tools and modern AI can significantly streamline the process of publishing your research. Journal finders are designed to identify the most appropriate journals for your manuscript. By analyzing the content of your research paper, these tools suggest journals that have previously published similar work, thereby increasing the likelihood of your manuscript being accepted.

11. **Review Author Guidelines:** Thoroughly review the author guidelines of your chosen journal. Ensure your manuscript adheres to their formatting, length, and submission requirements.

12. **Advanced AI tools:** AI-driven applications can assist in formatting your document according to journal-specific guidelines. AI tools are adept at improving the overall structure and style of your writing. They can provide suggestions for better organization, clarity, and coherence, making your manuscript more engaging and readable.

13. **Write a Compelling Cover Letter:** Draft a concise cover letter that highlights the significance of your research and its relevance to the journal's audience.

14. **Submit Manuscript Online:** Use the journal's submission system to upload your manuscript and associated documents. Complete all required fields accurately and follow any specific submission instructions.

15. **Monitor the Review Process:** Track the progress of your manuscript through the review process. Respond promptly to any requests for additional information or revisions from the reviewers or editors.

16. **Revise and Resubmit:** Address reviewer comments and revise your manuscript as needed. Prepare a detailed response letter outlining how each comment was addressed.

Closing Remarks on Becoming a Contributing Scholar

Embarking on the journey of writing a review paper is more than an academic exercise; it is an opportunity to contribute meaningfully to your field of study. As a scholar, your work has the potential to inspire, inform, and drive future research. The meticulous effort you put into synthesizing and analyzing literature reflects your dedication to advancing knowledge and fostering academic dialogue. Remember, every review paper you write adds a unique voice to the scholarly community. It demonstrates your ability to critically engage with existing research and provides a foundation for others to build upon. Embrace this responsibility with pride, knowing that your contributions are shaping the future of your discipline.

9. References

Allen Press. (n.d.). Narrative reviews: Flexible, rigorous, and practical. Retrieved from https://meridian.allenpress.com/jgme/article/14/4/414/484925/Narrative-Reviews-Flexible-Rigorous-and-Practical (Accessed: 31 November 2024).

Appinio. (n.d.). Meta-analysis. Retrieved from https://www.appinio.com/en/blog/market-research/meta-analysis (Accessed: 31 November 2024).

Batra, U., et al. (2024). AI-based pipeline for early screening of lung cancer: integrating radiology, clinical, and genomics data. The Lancet Regional Health - Southeast Asia, 24, 100352.

Becker, L. A. (2014). Writing for Social Scientists: How to Start and Finish Your Thesis, Book, or Article. University of Chicago Press.

Booth, A., Sutton, A., & Papaioannou, D. (2016). Systematic Approaches to a Successful Literature Review. Sage Publications.

Booth, W. C., Colomb, G. G., & Williams, J. M. (2008). The Craft of Research. University of Chicago Press.

Cestonaro, C., Delicati, A., Marcante, B., Caenazzo, L., & Tozzo, P. (2023). Defining medical liability when artificial intelligence is applied on diagnostic algorithms: a systematic review. Frontiers in Medicine, 10. https://doi.org/10.3389/fmed.2023.1305756.

Cooper, H., Hedges, L. V., & Valentine, J. C. (Eds.). (2009). The Handbook of Research Synthesis and Meta-Analysis (2nd ed.). Russell Sage Foundation.

Fink, A. (2019). Conducting Research Literature Reviews: From the Internet to Paper. Sage Publications.

Hart, C. (2018). Doing a Literature Review: Releasing the Research Imagination. Sage Publications.

HelpfulProfessor. (n.d.). Literature review examples. Retrieved from https://helpfulprofessor.com/literature-review-examples/ (Accessed: 31 November 2024).

Higgins, J. P. T., & Green, S. (Eds.). (2011). Cochrane Handbook for Systematic Reviews of Interventions (Version 5.1.0). The Cochrane Collaboration. Available from https://handbook-5-1.cochrane.org/ (Accessed: 31 November 2024).

Machi, L. A., & McEvoy, B. T. (2016). The Literature Review: Six Steps to Success. Corwin Press.

Mostofizadeh, S., & Tee, K.F. (2024). Review of next-generation earthquake-resistant geopolymer concrete. Discover Materials, 4, 62. https://doi.org/10.1007/s43939-024-00132-3.

Petticrew, M., & Roberts, H. (2006). Systematic Reviews in the Social Sciences: A Practical Guide. Blackwell Publishing.

Sanghavi, J. (2020). Review of smart healthcare systems and applications for smart cities. In A. Kumar & S. Mozar (Eds.), ICCCE 2019. Lecture Notes in Electrical Engineering (Vol. 570). Springer, Singapore. https://doi.org/10.1007/978-981-13-8715-9_39.

Sanghavi, J., & Kurhekar, M. (2024). Ocular disease detection systems based on fundus images: a survey. Multimedia Tools and Applications, 83, 21471–21496. https://doi.org/10.1007/s11042-023-16366-x.

Schimel, J. (2012). Writing Science: How to Write Papers That Get Cited and Proposals That Get Funded. Oxford University Press.

Scribbr. (n.d.). Systematic review methodology. Retrieved from https://www.scribbr.com/methodology/systematic-review/ (Accessed: 31 November 2024)

Sword, H. (2012). Stylish Academic Writing. Harvard University Press.

www.ingramcontent.com/pod-product-compliance
Lightning Source LLC
Chambersburg PA
CBHW040822120726
48005CB00012B/1483